# The LUNCHBOX Book

# The LUNCHBOX Book

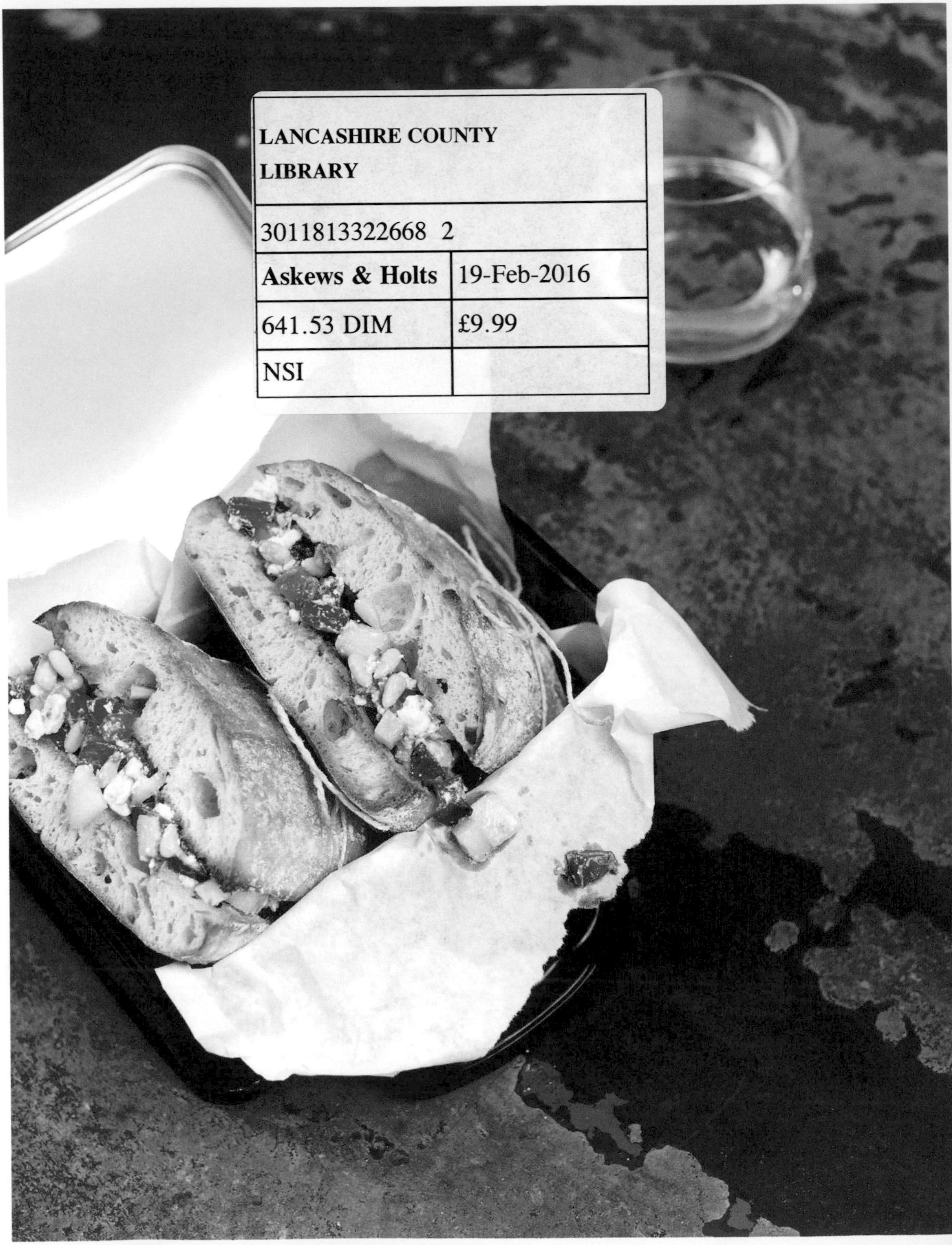

# CONTENTS

Greek
Ciabatta Sandwich
(see p40)

🕐 **PREPARATION TIME**
(not including baking and cooling times)

✏ **WHEN TO PREPARE**
morning or evening

● Enjoyed **COLD**
● Enjoyed **WARM**

# A LUNCHBOX
## IS LIKE A BOX OF
# CHOCOLATES.
## YOU NEVER KNOW WHAT YOU'RE GOING TO GET —

UNLESS YOU'VE PREPARED IT YOURSELF

# INTRODUCTION
## OR: HOW A LUNCHBOX
## CAN SAVE YOUR LIFE

**Many of us regularly eat meals outside the house, day after day. All too often in our hurried lunch breaks, or on the way to the station, we resort to overpriced and usually unhealthy ready meals, which lie heavily in our stomach and on our conscience.**

Of course, at times of stress it's not always possible to avoid situations where your breakfast consists of nothing more than a croissant tossed onto the car seat, or where you grab something for lunch at the snack bar opposite the office. But days like this should be the exception. Often, after a culinary lean period, you naturally feel like cooking something nice, enjoying your food, and feeling better as a result. Hopefully *The Lunchbox Book* can help you with that.

A healthy, balanced diet can be a source of stability in your life. What do I mean by that? In terms of my own life, in the last year I've experienced a lot of significant changes. After seven years we closed the little restaurant in Nuremberg that I ran together with my mother and my sister. That was a particularly hard step for me, because the restaurant was the start of my unexpected cooking career.

On the other hand, I had moved on, and now I was arranging dinners, small cooking events, and running cookery courses. Thanks to my cooking-related travel, it felt as though I had visited every single service station in the country. With all these new life situations and a multitude of projects, I sometimes find it really hard to keep the right balance. But it's exactly at these times I find it helps if I pay attention to my diet.

When I'm out and about, I'm always happy if I have home-made food in my lunchbox. It doesn't matter if it's a sandwich, some pasta, or a sweet snack. A lovingly filled lunchbox can be an oasis in everyday life, an anchor, or sometimes even a lifesaver. With this in mind, the recipes in this cookbook are designed to be quick and easy – things you can prepare with minimal effort in the morning or the night before, which can be enjoyed warm or cold, and are something to really look forward to.

Nothing boosts your flagging spirits more than the anticipation of a healthy meal, which will restore energy to body and soul and help you become full of beans again. So, get your lunchbox ready, steady, **GO!**

Love

Kat

# 5 ONE-SHOP LUNCHES!

Who has time to go shopping every day, in order to have the freshest possible produce on the table? Luckily, you don't need to. If you shop cleverly at the weekend, you can stock up with everything you need to fill your lunchbox with delicious meals the whole week long.

## YOU CAN COOK THESE 5 DISHES ...

**Apple Strudel Rice Pudding (see p24)**
with Almonds, Raisins, and Cinnamon

**Tomato Pilaf (see p70)**
with Feta and Coriander

**Greek Ciabatta Sandwich (see p40)**
with Feta and Pine Nuts

**Chickpea Chilli (see p84)**
with Basmati Rice

**Indian Vegetable Samosas (see p116)**
with Cucumber and Coriander Dip

## OR THESE 5 DISHES ...

**Pumpkin Rolls (see p127)**
with Rosemary and Almonds

**Glass Noodle Salad (see p75)**
with Green Beans, Roasted Chickpeas, Chilli, and Peanuts

**Pumpkin Muffins (see p123)**
with Feta, Pecans, and Thyme

**Peanut Butter Banana Oatmeal (see p20)**

**Carrot and Red Lentil Stew (see p88)**
with Coconut

## ... WITH THIS SHOPPING LIST

3 onions | 1 potato | 1 carrot | 1 cucumber | 2 peppers| 2 tomatoes | 2 chillies | fresh coriander| 1 apple | butter | 200g (7oz) quark or curd cheese | filo pastry | 80g (3oz) feta cheese | 3 pickled chilli peppers | 6 olives| frozen peas | 1 tin chickpeas | 1 tin chopped tomatoes | 1 jar passata | tomato purée | 160g (6oz) long-grain rice | 50g (2oz) basmati rice | almonds | raisins | ground cinnamon | vanilla pod | honey | pine nuts | dried oregano | curry powder | olive oil | 1 ciabatta roll

## ... IF THIS IS YOUR SHOPPING LIST

1 squash or pumpkin | handful of fine green beans | 2 onions | 1 carrot | 2 chillies| 1 banana | fresh coriander | fresh thyme | fresh rosemary | 500ml (16fl oz) milk | butter | 250g (9oz) quark or curd cheese | 120g (4½oz) feta cheese | filo pastry | 1 egg | 60g (2oz) glass noodles | 1 tin chickpeas | 70g (2½oz) red lentils | oats | plain flour | baking powder | raisins | flaked almonds | pecans | roasted peanuts | peanut butter | honey | tomato purée | coconut milk | olive oil | sesame oil

# LUNCHBOX TEAM

Just imagine if you only had to prepare a lunchbox once a week, but could still enjoy a different delicious lunch every day. The "lunchbox team" makes that possible: one colleague in turn prepares lunch for themselves and the rest of the team. This saves time; you can buy the ingredients more cheaply in larger quantities; and everyone gets to socialize together during lunch breaks.

## SHOPPING TIP

Many of the recipes in this book are designed for one person. So it's often a good idea to buy ingredients such as cheese, meat, fruit, and vegetables at the deli counter or the greengrocer's. This way, you can buy a small quantity at a time, and avoid having to waste anything.

## THE BASIC
# LUNCHBOX KIT

For anyone who's out and about a lot and doesn't have much time, there are a couple of simple tricks to ensure that there is always enough food in the house to magic up a dish for the following day, whatever the circumstances. Below is a list of the most important ingredients to help make filling your lunchbox quick and easy.

## IN THE CUPBOARD

potatoes
onions
bread (sliced bread)
UHT milk
pasta
grains
  (couscous,
  bulgur wheat)
rice
lentils
pumpkin and
  sunflower seeds

pine nuts
sesame seeds
chilli flakes
salt and pepper
chopped tomatoes
  (tinned)
passata (jar)
chickpeas (tinned)
pesto
semolina
oats
muesli

cornflakes
dried fruits
  (raisins,
  cranberries)
whole nuts
  (walnuts,
  almonds)
ground nuts
  (hazelnuts,
  almonds)
plain flour
baking powder

cocoa powder
chocolate
marzipan
chocolate spread
peanut butter
sugar
vanilla sugar
maple syrup
ground cinnamon
desiccated coconut
coconut milk

## IN THE FRIDGE

eggs
butter
cream cheese
natural yogurt
crème fraîche
plain tofu
jam
hard cheese
halloumi cheese

Camembert
feta cheese
olives (jar)
ketchup
mustard
pizza dough
filo pastry
puff pastry

## IN THE FREEZER

frozen bread rolls
frozen vegetables
  (peas, spinach,
  broccoli)
frozen herbs

# CLEVER PREPARATION
## & STORAGE

Whether it's a juicy filled sandwich, a colourful pasta dish, or a delicate salad, if the food is going to survive the journey unscathed, it must be packed carefully. By following these tips, you can guarantee an enjoyable meal from your lunchbox, day after day.

## SANDWICHES — PERFECTLY PROTECTED

As long as they're prepared carefully, sandwiches can still be fresh and appetizing, even after a long journey.

- **Wrap sandwiches, rolls, and bagels** in a large sheet of greaseproof paper or foil, and pack them in a re-usable plastic box, or a sandwich bag. Clingfilm is not suitable: it doesn't hold sandwiches tightly enough together, and if your sandwiches don't fall apart, they'll probably be soggy.
- **Don't make sandwiches until the morning**. But get your ingredients ready the night before, if possible. Keep toasted bread in a plastic container or wrapped in foil, and store the filling in the fridge. This will help your sandwich stay crispy on the outside and soft on the inside.
- **If you do make a sandwich in the evening**, store it, wrapped, in the fridge overnight. If it is unwrapped in the fridge, it will dry out, and by the next day it will have absorbed the flavours of whatever else is in your fridge.
- **Lettuce leaves, cucumber, tomatoes, and peppers** make sandwiches nice and moist. To prevent them making the bread soggy, dab them dry with kitchen paper before you make the sandwich. Tomatoes should ideally be deseeded.
- **Butter melts** outside of the fridge, so only spread it thinly on the bread. However, it also helps stop your bread absorbing too much moisture from the other ingredients.
- **Cheese and ham** prefer to be kept cool, and they can quickly go bad at high temperatures. So, in summer, make sure you keep sandwiches and salads in the fridge until ready to eat.
- **Brown bread** stays fresh and dry longer than white bread. If you've got a long day ahead of you, the best option is to go for wholemeal varieties.

## WARM DISHES AND SALADS FOR THE LUNCHBOX

Dishes which are cooked the evening before, such as breakfast porridge, soups, grain salads, pasta dishes, or potato salad, need special packaging treatment.

—  **Let warm dishes cool down properly** before putting them into a plastic container or sealing them in a jar. In a sealed container, warm food continues to cook, becoming overdone and mushy, and forming unappetizing condensation.
—  **Store dishes overnight in the fridge** – well sealed in a plastic box, or covered with a plate or foil.
—  **To help cool down warm dishes** in the fridge, stick a metal spoon in the food container. The metal conveys the cold quickly down to the base of the container, and the food will cool down more quickly.
—  **Sauces, dips, salad dressings, and cheese** for sprinkling should be stored separately, and only added to the dish just before eating. It looks tastier, and helps delicate ingredients such as lettuce leaves stay nice and crisp.

## FRUIT TO GO

—  **Fruits** that turn brown quickly, such as apples, pears, and apricots, also avocados, are best prepared shortly before eating. If that's not possible, don't worry. Brown fruit is just as delicious and healthy as freshly cut fruit – it just doesn't look quite so nice.
—  **Berries** such as raspberries, blackberries, blueberries, strawberries, and currants are perfect vitamin-kicks for when you're on the go. Just wash and pat them dry, then transport them protected in a plastic container. They stay fresh and juicy for hours.
—  **Shakes and smoothies** – prepare these vitamin bombs only in the morning, to make sure their healthy ingredients survive as long as possible.

# WHICH PACKAGING
## FOR WHICH FOODS?

### Paper Food Bags
Bread with jam or peanut butter, biscuits, and sweet buns keep well in one of these bags. But avoid using them for anything too greasy or moist, since you'll find it soaks through the paper.

### Plastic Boxes
Plastic boxes are true all-rounders. You can transport sandwiches, salads, dressings, soups, pasta, and cakes in them. Before you fill them with liquids, such as soup, make absolutely sure that the box is leakproof! Microwaveable containers are ideal. You can quickly heat up food at your workplace, without having to spend time decanting it into another container. Plastic boxes should be washed carefully after each use with hot water and washing up liquid, or cleaned in the dishwasher, to keep them free of germs.

## ALSO IMPORTANT
From an environmental point of view, reusable containers are the best choice.

### Plastic or Aluminium Cups
These are suitable for shakes and smoothies. If you're not sure whether the lid is watertight, a twist-top jar is also an option. Then just pour the shake into a drinking glass when you get to work.

### Clingfilm
Perfect airtight packaging for chopped fruit or vegetables. Clingfilm keeps it fresh for longer, and it won't go brown quite as quickly. Also suitable for biscuits and dry cakes.

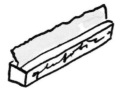

### Foil
Foil is used to wrap filled sandwiches, bagels, or wraps. The foil keeps things fresh, and the ingredients can't fall apart while they're being transported. Pastries are also well protected by wrapping in foil.

# MAKE THE MOST OF LEFTOVERS

It doesn't matter whether you're shopping for one person or many, every so often, there will be something left over. Which is not a bad thing, as leftovers are often a great base for conjuring up something new.

## BREAD AND ROLLS

From stale bread rolls you can make a delicious and succulent Greek sandwich, with a bit of olive oil, cucumber, and tomatoes (see p40). Leftover bread is also quickly transformed into crispy croutons, to use in salads such as A Kind of Waldorf Salad (see p58), for sprinkling onto soups or stews, or for snacking between meals. Equally delicious are the toasted strips of bread in a salad such as the Tomato and Bread Salad with Pesto and Pine Nuts (see p64).
**Storage:** Bread is best stored in the bread bin, never in the fridge or in a plastic bag.

## VEGETABLES

Fresh vegetables are the basis for most recipes, so leftover courgettes, carrots, and peppers are no problem. For example, courgettes: one day you can make a Grilled Cheese Sandwich with Courgette and Ricotta (see p39), and the next day Courgette Campanelle with Goat's Cheese and Thyme (see p98). If there are still leftovers after that, use them to liven up vegetable soups or stews, or add thin slices to a pizza.
**Storage:** Keep them in the fridge's vegetable compartment, and wrap chopped vegetables in a piece of foil.

## FRUIT

Got a couple of apples, bananas, or some berries left over? Chopped-up fruit or a few juicy berries are a welcome addition to muesli or your breakfast porridge. Meanwhile, apples can quickly be turned into a delicious Apple Strudel Rice Pudding with Almonds, Raisins, and Cinnamon (see p24). Of course, the classic recipe for leftover fruit is a compote: simply cut the fruit up small and let it simmer for a few minutes with a little water and sugar. A tart fruit compote goes perfectly with a recipe such as Honey Nut Waffles with Spelt and Cinnamon (see p147).

## CHEESE

If a couple of lonely cheese slices are left in the packet, these can be used up in an English Breakfast Roll with Cheddar, Scrambled Eggs, and Ham (see p44), or a One-Pot Cheeseburger Chilli (see p91). A block of hard cheese can simply be grated finely over pasta.
**Storage:** Soft cheese and cream cheese don't keep as long as hard cheese. Processed cheese can be kept significantly longer.

## HERBS

Herbs really liven up every dish. Just pop any leftovers into your next salad, perhaps the Courgette Parsley Couscous (see p69), or use them to enhance a salmon and cream cheese sandwich (see p46). The recipe specifies coriander, but what if you've only got parsley in the house? No problem: basil, parsley, and their cousins are flexible jacks of all trades. So just try out a different herb now and again, and your meals will be given a whole new dimension. Perhaps this creation will even become a new favourite!

# MUESLI & PORRIDGE

In the morning, after a night's sleep, the body's energy and nutritional reserves are depleted and need replenishing with liquid, protein, and carbohydrates. Starting the day is much easier with a tasty, healthy and, above all, filling breakfast – something you can look forward to, even the night before. A good breakfast also helps you concentrate on your work and avoid resorting to unhealthy snacking between meals.

These quick breakfast recipes can be spooned up and enjoyed either warm or cold. Because they consist of only grains, nuts, fruit, and dairy products, they give the body energy throughout the morning and don't lie heavily in the stomach. The muesli recipes can be made in the morning or the night before in a preserving jar or plastic container, and stored overnight in the fridge. They are easy to eat with a spoon, and no mess, whether you are breakfasting on a juddering train, at a motorway service station, or sitting at your desk.

🕐 EACH ABOUT 10 MIN.

✎ IN THE EVENING

● COLD

# PEANUT BUTTER BANANA OATMEAL

## FOR 1 PERSON

1 small banana
80g (3oz) oats
140ml (5fl oz) milk
1 tsp peanut butter
1 tsp runny honey
salt

Peel the banana and mash it well with a fork. Stir the oats, milk, peanut butter, honey, and a pinch of salt into the mashed banana. Cover the dish and let it sit overnight in the fridge.

# BLUEBERRY & ALMOND OATMEAL

## FOR 1 PERSON

80g (3oz) oats
140ml (5fl oz) milk
1 tsp desiccated
  coconut
1 tbsp dried cranberries
2 tbsp chopped
  almonds
1 tbsp runny honey
handful of blueberries

Mix together all the ingredients except the blueberries in a preserving jar or plastic container, and leave in the fridge. In the morning, scatter the blueberries over the oatmeal.

🕐 EACH ABOUT 15 MIN.

🔪 IN THE EVENING / MORNING

💧 COLD

## COTTAGE CHEESE MUESLI

Cottage cheese is a deliciously creamy, low-fat alternative to natural yogurt. It adds a subtle bite that will perk up any traditional muesli recipe, and offers a bit more protein to keep you going, too.

# MANGO MAPLE MUESLI

## FOR 1 PERSON

70ml (2½fl oz) milk

2 tbsp maple syrup

50g (1¾oz) oats

2 tbsp chopped
   cashew nuts

½ mango

100g (3½oz) cottage
   cheese

2 tbsp chopped
   pistachios

1 Heat the milk together with the maple syrup. Put the oats and cashew nuts in a bowl, pour over the milk, stir, and allow them to soak for about 10 minutes.

2 Meanwhile, peel the mango and cut the flesh into small cubes. Stir the cottage cheese into the muesli and scatter with the diced mango and pistachios.

# RASPBERRY MUESLI
## WITH SESAME AND PUMPKIN SEED CRUNCH

## FOR 1 PERSON

70ml (2½fl oz) coconut
   milk

2 tbsp runny honey

50g (1¾oz) oats

1 tbsp raisins

1 tbsp sesame seeds

1 tbsp pumpkin seeds

150g (5½oz) cottage
   cheese

small handful of
   raspberries

1 Heat the coconut milk with 1 tbsp honey. Put the oats and raisins in a bowl, pour over the milk, stir, and leave to soak for about 10 minutes.

2 Heat a dry frying pan. Add the sesame and pumpkin seeds and cook briefly, stirring. Add the rest of the honey, stir while heating, and then set the pan aside.

3 Add the cottage cheese to the oat mixture and stir well. Scatter the raspberries over the muesli and sprinkle with the sesame pumpkin seed crunch.

🕐 **ABOUT 35 MIN.**

✎ **IN THE EVENING**

◖◗ **WARM / COLD**

# APPLE STRUDEL RICE PUDDING
## WITH ALMONDS, RAISINS, AND CINNAMON

### FOR 1 PERSON

1 apple
½ vanilla pod
6 almonds
1 tsp butter
80g (3oz) long-grain
   rice
1 tbsp raisins
2 tbsp runny honey
ground cinnamon

Apple strudel rice pudding has little in common with a traditional rice pudding. The recipe uses long-grain rice, which means you don't have to stand forever at the stove, constantly stirring, to make sure it doesn't stick. It's so easy, it virtually cooks itself, and it tastes and smells just like a sweet, fruity, cinnamon-scented apple strudel with vanilla. Adding texture to this heavenly rice pudding is a sprinkling of juicy raisins and crunchy nuts.

1 Peel, quarter, and core the apples. Chop the fruit into cubes. Slice the vanilla pod lengthways and scrape out the seeds. Thinly slice the almonds.

2 Melt the butter in a pan. Add the rice, apple, vanilla seeds and pod, almonds, and raisins and cook for a few minutes. Stir in the honey and a generous pinch of ground cinnamon. Pour in 200ml (7fl oz) water.

3 Bring the mixture to the boil and let it simmer uncovered for about 10 minutes. Then remove the pan from the heat, stir, and cover. Let it stand for 20 minutes to finish cooking, then remove the vanilla pod.

🕐 **15 MIN.**

🔪 **IN THE EVENING / IN THE MORNING**

🌑 **WARM / COLD**

BREAKFAST BULGUR

# GRAPE BULGUR PORRIDGE
## WITH HONEY YOGURT AND WALNUTS

**FOR 1 PERSON**

80g (2½oz) bulgur
  wheat
100g (3½oz) Greek
  yogurt
1 tbsp runny honey
handful of grapes
2 tbsp chopped walnuts

1 Put the bulgur wheat into a bowl, pour over 160ml (5fl oz) boiling water, and stir. Let the bulgur wheat cook for about 10 minutes.

2 Stir the honey into the yogurt. Halve the grapes. Stir the honey yogurt and half the walnuts into the bulgur. Sprinkle with the grapes and the remaining walnuts.

**TRANSPORT TIP**
The milk bulgur porridge can be prepared directly in a plastic container.

# MILK BULGUR PORRIDGE
## WITH FIGS, DATES, AND ALMONDS

**FOR 1 PERSON**

2 dried figs
2 dried dates
5 almonds
80g (2½oz) bulgur wheat
1 tsp desiccated coconut
ground cinnamon
160ml (5fl oz) milk
1 tbsp runny honey
1 tbsp pomegranate
  seeds (optional)

1 Finely chop the figs and dates, then thinly slice the almonds. Mix in a bowl with the bulgur wheat, desiccated coconut, and a generous pinch of ground cinnamon.

2 Heat the milk and honey in a small saucepan. Pour this over the bulgur wheat and fruit mixture and stir well. Allow the bulgur wheat to cook for about 10 minutes. Finally, sprinkle with the pomegranate seeds (if using).

🕐 EACH ABOUT 15 MIN.

🔪 IN THE EVENING

🥄 WARM / COLD

SEMOLINA PORRIDGE

# COCONUT SEMOLINA PORRIDGE
## WITH PINEAPPLE, PISTACHIOS, AND HONEY

**FOR 1 PERSON**

150ml (5fl oz) milk

150ml (5fl oz) coconut
milk

40g (1½oz) fine
semolina

2 tbsp honey

1 tbsp roughly chopped
pistachios

3 tbsp finely diced
pineapple

ground cinnamon

1 Simmer the milk, coconut milk, semolina, and 1 tbsp of the honey in a small saucepan for about 5 minutes.

2 Mix together the pistachios, pineapple, remaining honey, and a pinch of cinnamon. Scatter over the semolina to serve.

# APRICOT AND VANILLA SEMOLINA PORRIDGE
## WITH ALMONDS

**FOR 1 PERSON**

5 dried apricots

8 almonds

½ vanilla pod

300ml (10fl oz) milk

40g (1½oz) fine
semolina

2 tbsp brown sugar

1 Chop the apricots and set aside a small quantity. Slice the almonds and reserve a few slices. Slice the vanilla pod lengthways and scrape out the seeds. Simmer the milk with the semolina, sugar, apricots, almonds, vanilla seeds and pod in a small saucepan for about 5 minutes.

2 Remove the vanilla pod, and serve the apricot and vanilla porridge, sprinkled with the reserved apricots and almonds.

### TRANSPORT TIP
The trifle looks amazing layered in a preserving jar. Or you can just place the ingredients next to each other in a plastic container – this makes it more like a muesli, but it tastes just as delicious!

EACH ABOUT 10 MIN.

IN THE MORNING

COLD

## BREAKFAST TRIFLES

These trifles are just as colourful as the traditional British layered dessert, but transformed into an exquisite, healthy breakfast version.

# GREEK YOGURT TRIFLE
## WITH BLACKBERRY COMPOTE & ALMOND GRANOLA

### FOR 1 PERSON

1 tsp butter
3 tbsp oats
1 tbsp chopped almonds
1 tbsp honey
80g (3oz) blackberries
1 tsp blackberry jam
150g (5½oz) Greek yogurt

1 For the granola, melt the butter in a small pan, add the oats and almonds, and cook for a few minutes until golden brown. Add the honey, mix everything together well, and remove the pan from the heat.

2 For the compote, mash the blackberries in a bowl and stir in the jam. Arrange the yogurt, compote, and almond granola in alternating layers in a glass.

# PEACH BISCOTTI TRIFLE
## WITH HONEY AND RICOTTA

### FOR 1 PERSON

1 peach
6 biscotti (cantuccini)
150g (5½oz) ricotta cheese
1 tbsp honey

Halve the peach, remove the stone, and dice the flesh. Finely chop the biscotti. Mix the ricotta cheese and honey together in a bowl. Arrange the honey ricotta mix, peach pieces, and biscotti in alternating layers in a glass.

# SHAKES

Breakfast shakes are healthy and very quick to make – perfect for anyone who has their breakfast standing up.

## ◊ AVOCADO YOGURT SHAKE

**FOR 1 PERSON**

½ avocado
4 dried dates
150g (5½oz) vanilla
  yogurt
100ml (3½fl oz) milk
1 tbsp honey

Peel, stone, and roughly chop the avocado. Chop the dates into small pieces and blend with the avocado, yogurt, milk, and honey until smooth.

AROUND 10 MIN.

IN THE MORNING

COLD

## PREPARATION TIP

If you don't have a food processor or blender, use a tall container and a hand-held blender.

# STRAWBERRY CHEESECAKE MILKSHAKE

**FOR 1 PERSON**

handful of strawberries
30g (1oz) cream cheese
150g (5½oz) natural yogurt
100ml (3½fl oz) milk
3 digestive biscuits
1 tbsp vanilla sugar
1 tbsp sugar

Hull the strawberries and blend all the ingredients together until smooth.

# SANDWICHES & WRAPS

Bread with some kind of topping has always been a lunchbox staple. It's filling and you don't have to eat it immediately – it still tastes good hours later. You can also make sure your lunch is nutritious, because if you prepare your own sandwich or roll, you know exactly what's in it. Even better, you rule out any nasty surprises, such as mountains of mayonnaise, or limp lettuce leaves.

   And a sandwich never gets boring! With a few tricks of the trade, you can transform it into something quite special, day after day – perhaps by creating a full English breakfast inside a bread roll, or by rolling a couple of healthy ingredients, such as lettuce and spicy beans, in a tortilla to make a wholesome wrap.

🕐  ABOUT 5 MIN.

🔪  IN THE EVENING

🫗  COLD

BREADS & ROLLS

A fresh ciabatta roll is tasty to start with, but it becomes something special when you fill it with the flavour combination of juicy sliced chicken, tangy Roquefort, and bitter radicchio leaves. Add some crunch with a sprinkling of pumpkin seeds.

# CHICKEN CIABATTA
## WITH ROQUEFORT, PUMPKIN SEEDS & RADICCHIO

## FOR 1 PERSON

1 ciabatta roll
2 radicchio leaves
40g (1½oz) Roquefort
   cheese
1 tsp pumpkin seeds
2 slices of chicken
3 slices of tomato

Slice the roll in half horizontally. Cut the radicchio into thin strips. Spread the Roquefort over the lower half of the roll and sprinkle with the pumpkin seeds. Arrange the radicchio, sliced chicken, and tomatoes on top. Replace the upper half of the roll and press down gently.

🕐  **ABOUT 15 MIN.**

🔪  **IN THE EVENING**

🌥  **WARM / COLD**

Halloumi is a superb cheese for sandwiches. It has a strong flavour and keeps its shape when cooked, unlike mozzarella cheese. Pair it with some crispy bread and fresh spinach leaves for this quick vegetarian kebab.

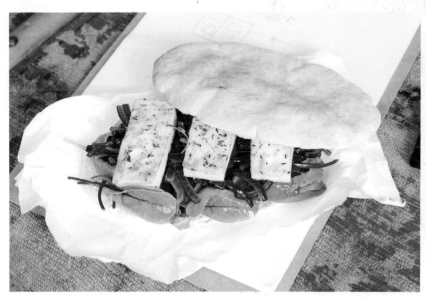

# HALLOUMI KEBAB
## WITH RED ONIONS AND SPINACH LEAVES

## FOR 1 PERSON

**1 pitta bread or flatbread, about 70g (2½oz)**
**1 small red onion**
**2 tsp oil**
**100g (3½oz) halloumi cheese**
**small handful of spinach leaves**

1  Crisp up the bread in the oven at 180°C (350°F/Gas 4) for about 5 minutes, then split it horizontally. Peel the onion and slice thinly. Heat 1 tsp of oil in a frying pan and sauté the onion, before setting it aside.

2  Cut the halloumi into three slices. Heat the remaining oil in the pan and fry the cheese until golden brown on both sides.

3  Scatter the spinach leaves over the lower half of the bread, followed by the onions and halloumi. Place the upper half of the bread on top and press down gently.

🕐  ABOUT 10 MIN.

🔪  IN THE EVENING/IN THE MORNING

🔴  WARM / COLD

BREADS & ROLLS

This sweet-savoury sandwich is irresistible. With its sautéed apple and softly melted Brie set off by tangy cranberry jam and full-flavoured, nutty bread, it tastes fantastic.

# APPLE WALNUT BREAD
## WITH BRIE AND CRANBERRIES

### FOR 1 PERSON

½ apple
50g (1¾oz) Brie cheese
½ tsp butter
1 tsp chopped walnuts
2 slices walnut bread
1 tsp cranberry jam

1  Core the apple. Chop the apple and Brie into small pieces. Heat the butter in a pan and sauté the apple for a few minutes. Mix in the Brie and walnuts and take the pan off the heat.

2  Spread a slice of walnut bread with the jam and add the apple and Brie filling. Place the other slice of bread on top and press down gently.

ABOUT 15 MIN.

IN THE EVENING

WARM / COLD

Roasted courgette,
creamy ricotta, and
aromatic thyme make
this sandwich quite
special. You can quickly
reheat it in the office
kitchen, but it tastes
just as good cold.

# GRILLED CHEESE SANDWICH
## WITH COURGETTE AND RICOTTA

### FOR 1 PERSON

**2 large slices of
   wholemeal bread**
**2 tbsp ricotta cheese**
**1 tsp finely chopped
   thyme**
**1 tsp pine nuts, toasted**
**salt and pepper**
**½ courgette**
**2 tbsp olive oil**

1 Remove the crusts from the bread. Mix together the ricotta,
thyme, and pine nuts, and season with salt and pepper. Slice
the courgette thinly lengthways.

2 Heat 1 tbsp olive oil in a frying pan, fry the courgette slices
on both sides until golden brown, and set aside. Spread
three-quarters of the ricotta mixture on one slice of bread,
lay the courgette slices on top, and season with salt and
pepper. Spread the other slice of bread with the remaining
ricotta mix, place it on top, and press down gently.

3 Heat the remaining olive oil in the pan and fry the sandwich
until golden brown on both sides.

ABOUT 15 MIN.

IN THE EVENING

WARM / COLD

# GREEK CIABATTA SANDWICH
## WITH FETA AND PINE NUTS

## FOR 1 PERSON

1 ciabatta roll
3 tsp olive oil
1 small tomato
½ small cucumber
6 olives, pitted
3 pickled chilli peppers
50g (1¾oz) feta cheese
1 tsp dried oregano
1 tsp pine nuts, toasted

Take a culinary short break to the Mediterranean: fresh, crunchy vegetables, aromatic herbs, tangy feta, and fruity olive oil together taste just like a Greek summer. This sandwich is perfect for the dreary days of winter, when holidays feel a long way off.

1 Preheat the oven to 180°C (350°F/Gas 4). Slice the ciabatta in half horizontally and drizzle the cut surfaces with 2 tsp olive oil. Bake the two halves of the roll directly on the middle oven shelf for a couple of minutes until crispy.

2 Deseed the tomato and dice the flesh finely. Peel and halve the cucumber, remove the seeds with a spoon, and then chop into small cubes. Finely chop the olives and chilli peppers. In a bowl, roughly mash the feta with a fork and stir in the chopped vegetables, the remaining olive oil, oregano, and pine nuts.

3 Spread the feta and vegetable mixture on the lower half of the roll. Place the upper half on top and press down gently.

## PREPARATION TIP

If you prepare the sandwich the evening before, make sure you bake the ciabatta roll until it is very crisp and then let it cool down fully. This helps prevent the filling from soaking into the bread.

🕐 **EACH ABOUT 10 MIN.**

✏️ **IN THE EVENING**

⬤ **COLD**

**BAGELS**

# HAM BAGEL
## WITH WILD GARLIC CREAM CHEESE & CRESS

### FOR 1 PERSON

1 bagel
1 small tomato
2 tbsp cream cheese
1 tsp wild garlic pesto
1 tsp sunflower seeds
2 slices cooked ham
½ small box of cress

**1** Split the bagel in half horizontally. Slice the tomatoes thinly, removing the core in the process. Mix the cream cheese with the pesto, spread on the bottom half of the bagel, and sprinkle with the sunflower seeds.

**2** Arrange the sliced tomato and ham on top and scatter with the chopped cress. Replace the top half of the bagel and press down gently.

# EGG MAYONNAISE BAGEL

### FOR 1 PERSON

1 bagel
1 tbsp crème fraîche
½ tsp mustard
1 tsp chopped chives
salt and pepper
1 hard-boiled egg
small handful of lamb's
  lettuce

**1** Split the bagel in half horizontally. Mix together the crème fraîche, mustard, chives, salt and pepper. Peel and chop the egg and add it to the mixture. Remove any stalks from the lamb's lettuce.

**2** Spread the egg mayonnaise over the lower half of the bagel and lay the lamb's lettuce on top. Replace the upper half of the bagel and press down gently.

ABOUT 15 MIN.

IN THE MORNING

WARM / COLD

# ENGLISH BREAKFAST ROLL
## WITH CHEDDAR, SCRAMBLED EGGS, AND HAM

### FOR 1 PERSON

1 slice of Cheddar cheese
1 small tomato
2 tsp butter
2 slices of ham
2 eggs
salt and pepper
1 bread roll

There's nothing finer than a traditional English breakfast of eggs, bacon, sausages, and beans. But time is usually too tight in the morning for such a feast. Now and then, treat yourself to this English breakfast roll with tangy Cheddar, scrambled eggs, tomatoes, and fried ham. It's quick to prepare and tastes just like the real thing.

1 Chop the Cheddar into small pieces. Slice the tomatoes, removing the core in the process. Heat 1 tsp of butter in a frying pan and fry the ham and tomato slices on both sides. Remove and set aside.

2 Heat the remaining butter in the pan. Whisk the eggs, pour them into the pan, and sprinkle over the Cheddar. Let the eggs thicken, stirring all the time, and season with salt and pepper.

3 Slice the roll in half horizontally, lay the ham and tomato slices on it and spread the scrambled eggs on top. Replace the upper half of the roll and press down gently.

🕐 EACH ABOUT 10 MIN.

🔪 IN THE MORNING

⬤ COLD

## TRAMEZZINI

Snow-white Italian tramezzini bread, velvety and slightly sweet, tastes like nothing else. If you can't get hold of it, regular white sliced bread, with the crusts removed, is a good substitute for making these elegant sandwiches.

# CUCUMBER TRAMEZZINI
## WITH MUSTARD AND DILL BUTTER

### FOR 1 PERSON

2 tsp butter, softened
½ tsp mustard
1 tsp finely chopped dill
salt and pepper
2 large slices of
 tramezzini bread
1 piece of cucumber,
 about 3cm (1¼in) long

Cucumber sandwiches are a traditional British classic, and this recipe – butter, dill, juicy cucumber slices, and a hint of mustard – is fit for a queen.

1 Stir the butter, mustard, dill, and seasoning together with a fork. Spread this mixture thinly onto both slices of tramezzini bread.

2 Peel the cucumber, slice it thinly, and arrange it on top of one slice of bread. Put the other tramezzini slice on top and press down gently.

# SALMON TRAMEZZINI
## WITH TOMATOES, CREAM CHEESE, AND CRESS

### FOR 1 PERSON

½ tomato
1½ tbsp cream cheese
salt and pepper
2 large slices of tramezzini
 bread
3 slices of smoked salmon
2 romaine lettuce leaves
1 tbsp cress

1 Core and deseed the tomato and chop it into small cubes. Combine it with the cream cheese and a little salt and pepper.

2 Spread the tramezzini slices thinly with the tomato and cream cheese mixture. Place the salmon and lettuce leaves on one slice and scatter with cress. Place the other tramezzini slice on top and press down gently.

🕐 EACH ABOUT 10 MIN.

🔪 IN THE MORNING

⬤ COLD

# PARMA HAM TRAMEZZINI
## WITH GORGONZOLA CREAM AND ROCKET

### FOR 1 PERSON

1 tbsp Gorgonzola cheese
1 tbsp cream cheese
2 large slices of tramezzini
  bread
2 slices Parma ham
small handful of rocket
1 tsp sunflower seeds

[1] Crumble the Gorgonzola and combine with the cream cheese. Spread this mixture onto both slices of tramezzini. Cover one slice with ham. Arrange the rocket on top and sprinkle with the sunflower seeds. Place the other tramezzini slice on top and press down gently.

# CHOCOLATE AND BANANA TRAMEZZINI
## WITH COCONUT AND PEANUT BUTTER

### FOR 1 PERSON

½ banana
2 large slices of
  tramezzini bread
1 tsp chocolate hazelnut
  spread
1 tsp peanut butter
½ tsp desiccated coconut

This tramezzini tastes sweet and nutty, and yet at the same time exotically fruity thanks to the desiccated coconut and banana. La dolce vita in the form of a sandwich!

[1] Thinly slice the banana. Spread one slice of tramezzini with the chocolate spread and the other with the peanut butter. Lay the banana on one tramezzini slice and sprinkle with desiccated coconut. Place the other tramezzini slice on top and press down gently.

## TIPS FOR THE PERFECT TRAMEZZINI

[1] Always pat dry lettuce, tomatoes, and similar ingredients before using, so that the bread doesn't get soggy.

[2] Tramezzini bread dries out quickly. So wrap the prepared sandwich well in foil.

[3] Ideally, don't prepare the tramezzini until the morning. If you do have to prepare it the night before, toast the bread beforehand, as this will help to delay the moisture penetrating the bread.

🕐 **ABOUT 15 MIN.**

✎ **IN THE EVENING**

◖ **WARM / COLD**

**PACKING TIP**
Place a sheet of greaseproof paper on a larger sheet of foil. Lay the burrito on top and then wrap it up securely.

# HOT BEAN BURRITO
## WITH AVOCADO

### FOR 1 PERSON

½ pepper
2 tbsp kidney beans
   (tinned), drained
1 tbsp sweetcorn
   (tinned), drained
1 tbsp spicy ketchup
1 tsp finely chopped
   parsley
salt and pepper
½ avocado
1 large tortilla wrap
handful of mixed salad
   leaves

1 Remove the stalk and seeds and chop the pepper into small cubes. In a bowl, mix the pepper pieces with the beans, ketchup, and parsley. Season with salt and pepper. Peel the avocado and slice the flesh.

2 Lay out the wrap (see photo on p48 and tip above). Cut the salad leaves into strips, lay them vertically down the middle of the wrap, and spread the bean mixture on top. First fold over the upper and lower edges of the wrap, then the right and left sides. Roll up the burrito tightly along one edge.

### ≈◇ MAKE IT HOT ◇≈

If you like your burrito hot, you can heat the bean mixture in a small saucepan and also warm up the tortilla wrap in the oven.

## VEGETABLE VARIATIONS
A flatbread or focaccia sandwich is ideal for using up leftovers. For another quick filling, try sautéed antipasti from a jar, such as aubergine or peppers.

🕐 **ABOUT 20 MIN.**

🔪 **IN THE EVENING**

🌗 **WARM / COLD**

# ARTICHOKE AND COURGETTE FOCACCIA
## WITH RED PESTO & MOZZARELLA

This sandwich is bursting with vegetables. It has a spicy flavour, it's easy to digest, and it really fills you up. Instead of the Italian focaccia, try making it with a Turkish or Greek flatbread.

## FOR 1 PERSON

¼ focaccia or flatbread
2 tsp red pesto
1 tsp finely chopped
  parsley
70g (2½oz) mozzarella
  cheese
½ courgette
4 artichoke hearts
  (from a jar)
2 tbsp olive oil
salt and pepper

1 Preheat the oven to 180°C (350°F/Gas 4). Split the focaccia in half horizontally. Spread the pesto onto the lower half and scatter with parsley. Tear the mozzarella into small pieces and arrange on top. Lay both halves of the bread directly on the middle oven shelf, cut sides uppermost, and let them crisp up for about 10 minutes.

2 In the meantime, slice the courgette lengthways into thin strips. Cut the artichokes in half. Heat the olive oil in a frying pan and fry the courgette slices on both sides. Add the artichokes and cook together briefly with the courgette. Season with salt and pepper and set aside to cool.

3 Arrange the courgette and artichokes on the lower half of the focaccia. Place the upper half on top and press down gently.

⏰ EACH ABOUT 10 MIN.

🔪 IN THE EVENING

🔵 WARM / COLD

## QUESADILLAS

Quesadillas are the perfect lunchtime snack. These delicious wraps can be prepared in zero time and with little effort, taste just as good warm or cold, and can be filled with a wide array of ingredients.

# VEGETABLE QUESADILLA
## WITH MOZZARELLA

**FOR 1 PERSON**

½ pepper
1 spring onion
½ tomato
oil
1 tortilla wrap
3 tbsp grated
  mozzarella cheese
salt and pepper

1 Remove the seeds from the pepper and dice the flesh. Trim the root and outer leaves from the spring onion, and slice the bulb into thin rings. Core, deseed, and dice the tomato.

2 Spread a couple of drops of oil around a non-stick frying pan using kitchen paper. Heat the pan, place the tortilla in it, and arrange the vegetables and mozzarella on one half. Season with salt and pepper. Fold the wrap over in a half-moon shape. Fry the quesadilla on both sides over a low heat until golden brown. Remove from the pan and cut in half.

# GOAT'S CHEESE &
# SPINACH QUESADILLA
## WITH PINE NUTS

**FOR 1 PERSON**

oil
1 tortilla wrap
handful of baby
  spinach
3 tbsp grated goat's
  cheese
1 tbsp pine nuts,
  toasted
salt and pepper

Spread a couple of drops of oil around a non-stick frying pan using kitchen paper. Heat the pan, place the tortilla in it and arrange the spinach and goat's cheese on one half. Sprinkle with the pine nuts and season with salt and pepper. Fold the wrap over in a half-moon shape. Fry the quesadilla on both sides over a low heat until golden brown. Remove from the pan and cut in half.

ABOUT 25 MIN.

IN THE EVENING

WARM / COLD

# VEGETARIAN LAHMACUN
## WITH TOFU & SOURED CREAM

This quick, veggie version of the Turkish snack is spicy, but also pleasantly refreshing, thanks to the crunchy salad and soured cream. Protein-packed tofu helps refuel you for the second half of the day.

## FOR 1 PERSON

½ onion
½ pepper
½ chilli
50g (1¾oz) plain tofu
1 tbsp olive oil
1½ tbsp tomato purée
1 tbsp finely chopped
   coriander
salt and pepper
½ tomato
small handful of iceberg
   lettuce
1 tortilla wrap
2 tbsp soured cream

1  Peel the onion and dice it finely. Destalk and deseed the pepper and chilli. Dice the pepper and finely chop the chilli. Gently squeeze out any excess moisture from the tofu and crumble it. Heat the olive oil in a small pan. Sauté the onion, tofu, pepper, chilli, and tomato purée for a few minutes. Add 4 tbsp water and simmer until the water has evaporated. Stir in the coriander and season the tofu mixture with salt and pepper.

2  Core and deseed the tomato and dice it finely. Cut the lettuce into thin strips.

3  Lay out the wrap (see photo on p48 and tip on p49). Spread the tofu mixture over the wrap and arrange the lettuce and tomato in a strip down the middle. Drizzle the soured cream over the lettuce and tomato. Fold over the lower end of the lahmacun, then fold the left and right sides in to the centre.

# SALADS

Salad is one of the best types of lunch, for all sorts of reasons. Choose your ingredients and garnishes carefully, and a salad can fill you up until evening, while avoiding that sleepy, post-lunch slump. What's more, they're fun to prepare, and easy to transport in a plastic container. Salad doesn't have to be endless versions of green leaves and dressing, either. There are any number of variations on the humble salad – perhaps with couscous, bulgur wheat, or noodles as a base. Or how about a new interpretation of the classic potato salad? This chapter is full of interesting, sophisticated recipes that will inspire you to pack a healthy and filling salad in your lunchbox.

⏱ EACH ABOUT 15 MIN.

🔪 IN THE EVENING

🔵 COLD

# SALAD LIKE THEY SERVE IN NICE

## FOR 1 PERSON

3 tbsp olive oil

1 tsp white balsamic
  vinegar

½ tsp mustard

1 tsp runny honey

salt and pepper

3 artichoke hearts (from
  a jar)

small handful of fine
  green beans

1 hard-boiled egg

large handful of romaine
  lettuce

1 tsp grated Parmesan
  cheese

1 tsp sunflower seeds

1 For the dressing, in a small bowl whisk together 1 tbsp olive oil with the vinegar, mustard, honey, salt, pepper, and around 1 tbsp water.

2 Halve the artichoke hearts and the beans, trimming the ends. Heat the remaining olive oil in a small pan and fry the beans for a couple of minutes until al dente. Shortly before the end of the cooking time, add the artichokes and fry together, then season the mixture with salt and pepper.

3 Peel and quarter the egg. Tear the salad leaves into bite-sized pieces and drizzle with the dressing. Top the salad with the bean and artichoke mixture and the egg, then sprinkle with Parmesan and sunflower seeds.

# A KIND OF WALDORF SALAD

## FOR 1 PERSON

1 tbsp Gorgonzola cheese

2 tbsp Greek yogurt

1 tsp olive oil

salt and pepper

small handful of red seedless
  grapes

large handful of mixed salad
  leaves

2 tbsp roughly chopped
  walnuts

1 tbsp croutons

1 For the dressing, mash the Gorgonzola with a fork in a small bowl and add the yogurt, olive oil, salt, pepper, and around 1 tbsp water, mixing well.

2 Halve the grapes lengthways. Tear the salad leaves into bite-sized pieces and drizzle with the dressing. Scatter over the grapes, walnuts, and croutons.

### TRANSPORT TIP

Carry the dressing separately in a well-sealed plastic container or small bottle and only dress the salad just before eating.

# POTATO

Potatoes are one of our favourite vegetables, whether it's crisp home-made chips, velvety mash, or buttery new potatoes, steamed in their skins. With potatoes you can conjure up an endlessly varied array of recipes for your lunchbox, including some delicious salads – just like the three pictured here (recipes are on the following pages). Potato salads have all sorts of advantages: they are quick to prepare, they travel well in a plastic container, and they even develop in flavour if they are prepared in advance.

# SALADS

3

## TRANSPORT TIP

Transport the Lime Curry Dip (see p63) separately and only add to the potatoes shortly before eating – this helps them stay nice and crispy.

1 Sweet Potato and Mango Salad
2 Herby Potato Salad
3 Roasted Potato and Chickpea Salad

⏱ **ABOUT 20 MIN.**

🔪 **IN THE EVENING**

🌓 **WARM / COLD**

## FOR 1 PERSON

1 sweet potato, about
   300g (10oz)
1 tbsp oil
½ tsp ground turmeric
salt
1 spring onion
1 tbsp finely chopped
   coriander
2 tbsp mango chutney
   (from a jar)

POTATO SALADS

# SWEET POTATO AND MANGO SALAD
### WITH SPRING ONIONS

This Indian-influenced potato salad is an absolute favourite. Oven-roasting the sweet potatoes makes them deliciously crispy and tender. Combined with fruity mango chutney, fresh coriander, and spring onions, this salad is a real explosion of flavours.

**1** Preheat the oven to 200°C (400°F/Gas 6). Line a baking tray with greaseproof paper. Peel the sweet potato, quarter it, and slice into ½cm (¼in) thick discs. Put the potato slices in a bowl and combine with the oil, turmeric, and a touch of salt. Then arrange on the baking tray and roast on the middle shelf for about 15 minutes, until golden brown.

**2** Remove the root and green outer leaves of the spring onion. Thinly slice the onion. Mix the potatoes in a bowl with the spring onion, coriander, and mango chutney.

⏱ **ABOUT 25 MIN.**

🔪 **IN THE EVENING**

🌓 **WARM / COLD**

# HERBY POTATO SALAD
### WITH OLIVE OIL AND SUGARSNAP PEAS

This potato salad is a treat for all fans of light Mediterranean cuisine. Aromatic herbs, crunchy sugarsnap peas, and a flavoursome olive oil provide the dish with a fresh-tasting, spring-like quality.

## FOR 1 PERSON

300g (10oz) small
  potatoes
handful of sugarsnap
  peas
large handful of lamb's
  lettuce
3 tbsp olive oil
1 tsp finely chopped
  thyme
1 tbsp chopped parsley
salt and pepper

1 Cook the potatoes, unpeeled, in salted water for about 15 minutes, until they are soft. Drain the potatoes, blanch in cold water, peel, and cut in half. Trim the ends of the sugarsnap peas, and the stalks of the lamb's lettuce. Put the lamb's lettuce into a bowl.

2 Heat 2 tbsp oil in a non-stick frying pan and fry the potatoes for a few minutes until lightly golden. Add the sugarsnap peas and continue frying until the sugarsnaps are cooked and the potatoes are golden brown.

3 Add the thyme, parsley, and remaining olive oil to the potato and sugarsnap peas. Season with salt and pepper and arrange on the lamb's lettuce.

🕐   ABOUT 20 MIN.
✎   IN THE EVENING
◖   WARM / COLD

## FOR 1 PERSON

300g (10oz) small
  potatoes
2 tbsp sesame oil
½ tsp ground turmeric
salt
4 tbsp chickpeas
  (tinned)
2 tbsp crème fraîche
½ tsp grated lime zest
½ tsp curry powder

# ROASTED POTATO
# AND CHICKPEA SALAD
## WITH LIME CURRY DIP

1 Preheat the oven to 200°C (400°F/Gas 6). Line a baking tray with greaseproof paper. Wash and pat dry the potatoes and slice thinly, leaving their skins on. Mix 1 tbsp sesame oil with the turmeric and salt. Toss the potatoes in a bowl with the turmeric oil.

2 Spread the potatoes over the baking tray and roast on the middle oven shelf for about 15 minutes. Halfway through the cooking time, add the chickpeas to the potatoes, stir them together, and and let them continue to cook.

3 For the dip, stir the lime zest, remaining sesame oil, and curry powder into the crème fraîche, and serve alongside.

🕐 **ABOUT 20 MIN.**

🔪 **IN THE EVENING**

🌡 **COLD**

# TOMATO BREAD SALAD
## WITH PESTO & PINE NUTS

Ciabatta toasted in olive oil is used for this salad, but you can use any type of bread you have left over. In no time, you'll have conjured up a superb tomato salad to which the basil pesto and crispy bread pieces add something quite special.

## FOR 1 PERSON

**1 stale ciabatta roll**
**4 tbsp olive oil**
**1 tsp green pesto**
**1 tsp white balsamic vinegar**
**salt and pepper**
**pinch of sugar**
**1 tsp capers (from a jar)**
**3 tomatoes**
**½ small cucumber**
**small handful of green salad leaves**
**1 tsp pine nuts, toasted**
**2 tsp Parmesan cheese shavings**

**1** Split the roll in half horizontally and cut into slices about 1cm (½in) thick. Heat 3 tbsp olive oil in a frying pan and fry the bread pieces on both sides until golden brown

**2** For the dressing, mix the pesto with the remaining olive oil, vinegar, and about 1 tsp water in a small bowl. Add the sugar and season to taste with salt and pepper.

**3** Roughly chop the capers. Cut the tomatoes into small pieces, removing the core. Peel the cucumber, cut it in half horizontally, and slice thinly. Tear the salad into bite-sized pieces and mix with the capers, tomatoes, cucumber, pine nuts, Parmesan, the dressing, and the bread pieces. Season with salt and pepper.

### TRANSPORT TIP

To keep the bread nice and crunchy, only add it to the salad shortly before eating. If it's well packed in a plastic container or wrapped in foil, it should stay crisp. Transport the dressing separately too, and add at the last moment.

**TASTY TOGETHER**

Crusty white bread is a great accompaniment to tabbouleh.

⏱ **ABOUT 20 MIN.**

🔪 **IN THE EVENING**

☁ **WARM / COLD**

# PUMPKIN AND PEARL BARLEY TABBOULEH
## WITH TAHINI, CRANBERRIES, AND PUMPKIN SEEDS

## FOR 1 PERSON

60g (2oz) pearl barley
salt and pepper
2 tbsp dried cranberries
200g (7oz) pumpkin or
   squash, such as Red
   Kuri or butternut
1 tbsp oil
2 tsp tahini (sesame
   paste)
1 tbsp pumpkin seeds
1 tbsp finely chopped
   parsley

Tahini is a sesame paste used in Middle Eastern cuisine. You can find it in healthfood shops and well-stocked supermarkets. It can transform a recipe into an aromatic, nutty dish, reminiscent of the Arabian Nights!

1 Cook the pearl barley in boiling salted water, according to the instructions on the packet, for about 15 minutes, until al dente.

2 In the meantime, roughly chop the cranberries. Peel the squash or pumpkin if necessary, then cut into small cubes. Heat the oil in a pan and sear the squash on all sides. Pour in about 80ml (2½fl oz) water and simmer until the water has evaporated and the squash is soft.

3 Drain the pearl barley and mix with the squash, cranberries, tahini, pumpkin seeds, and parsley. Season the tabbouleh with salt and pepper.

## TRY IT THIS WAY TOO
Instead of pearl barley, try using bulgur wheat, couscous, or rice.

## TRANSPORT TIP

Carry the lemon yogurt
separately in a small bottle
or plastic container.

⏱ **ABOUT 25 MIN.**

🔪 **IN THE EVENING**

☁ **WARM / COLD**

# COURGETTE PARSLEY COUSCOUS
## WITH FRIED SESAME CHEESE & LEMON YOGURT

## FOR 1 PERSON

50g (1¾oz) couscous
salt and pepper
3 tbsp natural yogurt
1 tsp runny honey
½ tsp lemon zest
1 tbsp breadcrumbs
1 tbsp sesame seeds
2 tbsp plain flour
1 egg
about 80g (3oz) feta
   cheese
½ courgette
4 tbsp olive oil
1 tbsp pine nuts,
   toasted
1 tbsp finely
   chopped parsley

1 Put the couscous and a pinch of salt into a bowl and pour over 120ml (4fl oz) of boiling water. Stir and leave to absorb for about 10 minutes. Meanwhile, make the lemon yogurt by mixing together the yogurt, honey, and lemon zest.

2 For the sesame cheese, mix the breadcrumbs with the sesame seeds and spread onto a plate. Spread the flour onto a second plate. In a small bowl whisk the egg and a little pepper with a fork. Cut the feta into four cubes and dip first in the flour, then the egg, and finally in the sesame breadcrumb mixture.

3 Chop the courgette into small cubes. Heat half the oil in a pan and fry the courgette in it. Stir in the couscous, pine nuts, and parsley. Season with salt and pepper and tip into a bowl.

4 Heat the remaining oil in a small pan, fry the feta cubes until golden brown on all sides, and arrange them on top of the couscous. Serve with the lemon yogurt.

ABOUT 25 MIN.

IN THE EVENING

WARM / COLD

# TOMATO PILAF
## WITH FETA AND CORIANDER

---

This pilaf is a bit like the delicious tomato rice dish served in Greek restaurants, which always tastes wonderfully of a Mediterranean holidays. A simple rice dish, it practically cooks itself, and smells deliciously spicy and fragrant with fresh herbs.

1 Peel and dice the onion. Chop the tomato into small cubes, removing the core. Remove the stalk and seeds from the pepper and chillies. Dice the pepper and slice the chilli into fine rings.

2 Heat the olive oil in a small saucepan and add the onion, tomato, pepper, chilli, rice, and tomato purée. Fry the vegetables briefly, stirring constantly. Add 200ml (7fl oz) of water, bring to the boil, and add a generous pinch of salt and pepper. Let the pilaf simmer for about 10 minutes. Remove from the heat, stir in the coriander, cover the pan, and let the rice continue cooking for about 10 minutes. Serve the pilaf with the feta crumbled over.

## FOR 1 PERSON

1 small onion
1 tomato
½ pepper
1 small chilli
2 tbsp olive oil
80g (3oz) long-grain rice
1 tbsp tomato purée
salt and pepper
2 tbsp finely chopped coriander
30g (1oz) feta cheese

## RING THE CHANGES

Try using courgette or aubergine instead of – or in addition to – the peppers.

🕐 **ABOUT 20 MIN.**

✎ **IN THE EVENING**

⬤ **WARM / COLD**

# NORTH AFRICAN CHICKEN AND QUINOA SALAD
## WITH SPINACH, DATES, PISTACHIOS, AND POMEGRANATE

## FOR 1 PERSON

60g (2oz) quinoa
salt and pepper
4 dried dates
1 chicken breast, about
  150g (5½oz)
2 tbsp oil
1 tbsp runny honey
handful of baby spinach
1 tbsp roughly chopped
  pistachios
2 tbsp pomegranate
  seeds

Quinoa, also known as Inca corn, looks like a combination of couscous and rice. It contains significantly more minerals than traditional grains, and is a great source of protein too. Quinoa is not just extremely healthy, it also tastes fantastic.

1 Bring the quinoa to the boil in a saucepan with 180ml (6fl oz) of water and a pinch of salt, and let it simmer for a couple of minutes. Then cover and let the quinoa cook on a low heat for about 10 minutes.

2 In the meantime, chop the dates into small pieces. Wash and pat dry the chicken breast, and chop into bite-sized pieces. Heat the oil in a pan and sear the meat on all sides. Reduce to a moderate heat, drizzle over the honey, and fry the chicken pieces until cooked through and golden brown.

3 Mix the warm quinoa with the dates, chicken, spinach, pistachios, and pomegranate seeds. Season with salt and pepper.

### TRY IT THIS WAY TOO
If you can't find quinoa, use couscous or bulgur wheat instead.

### PREPARATION TIP
If you like it nutty, just stir 2 tsp tahini or peanut butter into the salad.

⏲ ABOUT 20 MIN.

🔪 IN THE EVENING

🌡 WARM / COLD

# GLASS NOODLE SALAD
## WITH GREEN BEANS, ROASTED CHICKPEAS, CHILLI, AND PEANUTS

## FOR 1 PERSON

handful of fine green
 beans
60g (2oz) glass noodles
1 small chilli
2 tbsp sesame oil
4 tbsp chickpeas (tinned)
1 tbsp finely chopped
 coriander
1 tbsp roasted peanuts
salt and pepper

Glass noodles are extremely practical: just pour over boiling water, and within a few minutes they are cooked and ready to eat. These almost translucent noodles are perfect for lunch, since they are easily digested and go well with an array of different ingredients and flavours.

1 Cut the beans in half, trimming off the ends. Put the glass noodles into a bowl, place the beans on top, and cover the whole lot with boiling water. Gently separate the glass noodles with a fork. After 3 minutes, remove the beans and put them on a plate. Drain the glass noodles in a sieve and blanch them in cold water.

2 Remove the stalk and seeds from the chilli and slice into fine rings. Heat the sesame oil in a pan and cook the chickpeas in the oil for a few minutes until golden brown. Add the beans and chilli to the pan and fry them briefly with the chickpeas, before stirring in the glass noodles, coriander, and peanuts. Season the salad with salt and pepper.

**SUPER TIP**
Drizzle a bit of soy sauce over this colourful glass noodle salad to give it more of an Asian flavour.

ABOUT 20 MIN.

IN THE EVENING

WARM / COLD

# SWEET AND SOUR NOODLES
## WITH CHICKEN AND VEGETABLES

## FOR 1 PERSON

1 chicken breast
½ pepper
3 mushrooms
10 sugarsnap peas
100g (3½oz) egg noodles
2 tbsp oil
1 tbsp chopped cashew nuts
2 tbsp chopped pineapple
2 tbsp light soy sauce
2 tbsp chilli sauce
salt and pepper

There is no quicker Asian recipe than these sweet and sour Chinese egg noodles. You can vary the vegetables according to what's in season and substitute tofu or extra vegetables for the chicken. A creative recipe for when you need to be spontaneous and speedy!

1 Cut the chicken breast into bite-sized pieces. Remove the stalk and seeds from the pepper, then chop it into small pieces. Trim the stalks from the mushrooms and slice the caps. Trim the ends from the sugarsnap peas and cut in half.

2 Put the noodles into a heatproof bowl and cover with boiling water. Let them cook for about 5 minutes, according to the instructions on the packet, stirring occasionally.

3 Meanwhile, heat the oil in a pan and sear the chicken pieces on all sides. Add the vegetables and continue to fry until the meat is cooked. Strain the water from the noodles and add them to the meat, along with the cashew nuts, pineapple, soy sauce, and chilli sauce. Mix everything well and season with salt and pepper.

⏱ **ABOUT 25 MIN.**

🔪 **IN THE EVENING**

🌫 **WARM / COLD**

# ROSEMARY AND OLIVE MEATBALLS
## WITH FENNEL TZATZIKI

---

## FOR 1 PERSON

½ small fennel bulb
1 tsp finely chopped dill
125g (4½oz) natural
   yogurt
1 tbsp olive oil
salt and pepper
8 black olives, pitted
150g (5½oz) minced
   beef
1 tbsp finely chopped
   rosemary
1 tbsp grated
   Parmesan cheese
2 tbsp breadcrumbs
2 tbsp oil

With a few simple ingredients, these beef meatballs are transformed into little pleasure bombs. Add some fresh rosemary, tangy olives, and a bit of Parmesan, and the cooking aromas alone are reminiscent of Mediterranean holidays. Served with a distinctive fennel tzatziki, they taste fresh and light.

1 For the fennel tzatziki, discard the stem and slice the fennel finely. Finely chop the slices. Mix together the fennel, dill, yogurt, and olive oil, and season with salt and pepper.

2 For the meatballs, finely chop the olives. In a bowl, combine the meat, olives, rosemary, Parmesan, breadcrumbs, and a generous pinch of salt and pepper. Knead the mixture together with your hands and shape into small balls.

3 Heat the oil in a frying pan and fry the meatballs until golden brown all over. Remove and drain on kitchen paper. Serve the meatballs with the fennel tzatziki.

## TASTY TOGETHER!
Flatbreads or pittas go perfectly with the Mediterranean meatball and tzatziki combination.

# STEWS & SOUPS

In winter, when it's cold and your feet are frozen by the time you get to work, or if you're not feeling great and a cold is brewing, your body instinctively craves warming soup. Or perhaps you feel like filling up with a hearty stew. This chapter is designed for exactly those kinds of days. It contains recipe ideas for some wonderfully warming stews and soups, which can be made with straightforward ingredients in no time at all, and easily reheated the next day.

⏱ **ABOUT 20 MIN.**

🔪 **IN THE EVENING**

🎨 **WARM / COLD**

# TOFU VEGETABLE RATATOUILLE
## WITH COUSCOUS

If you believe that a ratatouille has to cook slowly for hours, this recipe proves otherwise. It can be prepared quite quickly by simply sautéing the vegetables. The fried tofu gives the ratatouille a protein boost, while the filling couscous side dish almost cooks itself.

## FOR 1 PERSON

**100g (3½oz) plain tofu**
**2 tbsp oil**
**½ tsp ground turmeric**
**40g (1½oz) couscous**
**salt and pepper**
**handful of finely**
  **chopped vegetables**
  **(such as peppers,**
  **courgettes, and**
  **aubergine)**
**150g (5½oz) chopped**
  **tomatoes (tinned)**
**1 tbsp finely chopped**
  **parsley**

1　Chop the tofu into small pieces and mix with the oil and turmeric in a small bowl. Put the couscous into a bowl, pour over 80ml (3fl oz) of boiling water, add a pinch of salt, stir and leave to cook for about 10 minutes.

2　In the meantime, heat a pan and sauté the tofu on all sides. Add the vegetables and continue to cook until the tofu is lightly crisped. Add the tomatoes and 100ml (3½fl oz) of water, and leave to simmer until the liquid has reduced by half.

3　Season the ratatouille with salt and pepper. Stir in the parsley and serve the ratatouille with the couscous.

🕐 **ABOUT 15 MIN.**

🔪 **IN THE EVENING**

◖ **WARM / COLD**

# CHICKPEA CHILLI
## WITH BASMATI RICE

A classic, slow-cooked chilli con carne with minced beef and beans is a fine thing indeed. But for quick lunches, something a bit simpler is required. That's where this vegetarian chickpea chilli comes in – it contains only a few ingredients, is deliciously spicy, and extremely filling.

## FOR 1 PERSON

50g (1¾oz) basmati rice
salt and pepper
1 small onion
1 chilli
1 tbsp olive oil
200g (7oz) chickpeas
  (tinned)
½ tsp curry powder
200g (7oz) passata
  (from a jar)
1 tbsp finely chopped
  coriander

1 In a small saucepan bring the basmati rice briefly to the boil with 100ml (3½fl oz) of water and a pinch of salt, stir, then cover and remove from the heat, leaving it to cook for about 15 minutes.

2 Meanwhile, peel and dice the onion. Destalk and deseed the chilli and slice into fine rings. Heat the olive oil and sweat the onions in a small pan. Briefly sauté the chilli, drained chickpeas, and curry powder with the onions. Add the passata and 150ml (5fl oz) of water. Let the chilli simmer until the liquid is reduced by a half.

3 Stir in the coriander and season the chilli with salt and pepper. Serve with the basmati rice.

⏱ ABOUT 15 MIN.

✎ IN THE EVENING

◗ WARM / COLD

## THE QUICKEST
# BEAN AND SPINACH STEW
## IN THE WORLD

## FOR 1 PERSON

1 small onion
2 tbsp olive oil
200g (7oz) chopped tomatoes
   (tinned)
large handful of spinach
250g (9oz) butter beans
   (tinned)
1 tbsp finely chopped dill
salt and pepper

This delicious bean stew, which also contains spinach, juicy tomatoes, and aromatic dill, is hearty and filling – perfect for a winter's day. And it's incredible how quickly you can get it on the table!

1 Peel and dice the onion. Heat the olive oil in a saucepan and sauté the onions. Add the tomatoes, along with 150ml (5fl oz) of water, and leave to simmer until the liquid has nearly evaporated.

2 Meanwhile, chop the spinach roughly. Add the spinach, drained beans, and dill to the tomatoes. Let everything simmer until the spinach has wilted. Season the stew with salt and pepper.

## TASTY TOGETHER
A chunk of slightly acidic feta cheese is the perfect garnish for this delicious bean stew.

**ABOUT 20 MIN.**

**IN THE EVENING**

**WARM**

## FOR 1 PERSON

1 small onion
1 carrot
½ chilli
2 tbsp olive oil
70g (2½oz) red lentils
2 tbsp tomato purée
3 tbsp coconut milk
1 tbsp finely chopped
   coriander
salt and pepper

# CARROT AND RED LENTIL STEW
## WITH COCONUT

Lentil stew sounds like lunch in a hippie bedsit of the 1970s. But these delicious little pulses can also be used to conjure up tasty, modern dishes. Red lentils are used here, because they cook super quickly and have a pleasant, mellow taste. Using chilli, coconut milk, and coriander gives this dish an irresistible Asian touch.

1 Peel and dice the onion. Peel and finely slice the carrot. Remove the stalk and seeds from the chilli, then chop it finely. Heat the olive oil in a pan and sauté the onion, carrot, chilli, lentils, and tomato purée for a couple of minutes, stirring continuously.

2 Add sufficient water to just cover the lentil mixture. Let the stew come to the boil and then simmer for about 15 minutes. Then stir in the coconut milk and coriander. Season the stew with a generous pinch of salt and pepper.

ABOUT 20 MIN.

IN THE EVENING

WARM / COLD

# ONE-POT CHEESEBURGER CHILLI

**FOR 1 PERSON**

1 small onion
1 chilli
2 tbsp olive oil
150g (5½oz) minced beef
50g (1¾oz) pipe rigate
   (elbow macaroni)
150g (5½oz) passata
4 tbsp kidney beans
   (tinned)
2 tbsp finely chopped
   parsley
3 tbsp grated
   Emmental cheese
salt and pepper

A recipe designed for hectic, everyday life shouldn't just be quick to prepare, but should also avoid turning the entire kitchen upside down. This unique recipe, which combines two classic favourites – cheeseburger and chilli con carne – is quickly and easily cooked in a single pan.

1 Peel and dice the onion. Remove the stalk and seeds from the chilli and chop it finely. Heat the olive oil in a pan. Sauté the onion, chilli, and minced beef over a high heat until the meat juices have evaporated.

2 Stir in the pasta, passata, and 300ml (10fl oz) of water. Let the chilli simmer until the pasta is cooked al dente. If needed, add more water during cooking.

3 Stir in the beans, parsley, and Emmental, and season the chilli with salt and pepper.

**ABOUT 20 MIN.**

**IN THE EVENING**

**WARM**

# MULTICOLOURED MINESTRONE

## FOR 1 PERSON

1 small carrot
1 stick celery
small handful of fine
    green beans
2 tbsp olive oil
150g (5½oz) passata
    (from a jar)
60g (2oz) pipe rigate
    (elbow macaroni)
salt and pepper
1 tbsp grated
    Parmesan cheese
1 tsp finely chopped
    thyme

Minestrone is Italian cuisine's classic soup. And for good reason: minestrone can be prepared in no time, the ingredients are easy to get hold of, and, thanks to the pasta, it's really filling.

1　Peel and thinly slice the carrots. Remove the leaves from the celery and slice the stalk thinly. Trim the beans and cut them in half.

2　Heat the olive oil in a saucepan and sauté the vegetables briefly. Add the passata, 300ml (10fl oz) of water, and the pasta. Leave to simmer until the pasta is cooked, adding more water if necessary during cooking.

3　Season the minestrone generously with salt and pepper. Before eating, sprinkle with the Parmesan and thyme.

### TRY IT THIS WAY TOO

There are no vegetables or pasta shapes that don't work in minestrone. So it's the perfect recipe to use up leftovers or to go wild with your imagination!

# PASTA

If time is short and something filling is needed, most people instinctively opt for a pasta dish. And that's not a bad idea, because carbohydrate-rich pasta fills you up quickly, is low in fat – and tastes great. However, there are a few things to be aware of if you want to pack a pasta meal in your lunchbox. Most importantly, steer clear of rich sauces. These lie heavily in the stomach and increase the risk of spills if you're eating on the go. Instead, a splash of olive oil, a knob of butter, or some grated Parmesan cheese, along with some well-chosen vegetables and herbs, make for a healthier, less messy pasta lunch.

What's more, while pasta does make you happy, too much of it can make you feel tired and sluggish. So it's important to get the right balance between the pasta and other ingredients. The more fresh vegetables the recipe contains, the more easily digestible it is – and you can enjoy your meal confident that you won't soon be suffering the dreaded post-lunch slump.

ABOUT 20 MIN.

IN THE EVENING

WARM / COLD

# BROCCOLI BOWS
## WITH SAUTÉED SALMON AND DILL

## FOR 1 PERSON

100g (3½oz) farfalle
(bow-shaped pasta)
salt and pepper
handful of broccoli
florets
1 salmon fillet, about
100g (3½oz)
1 tbsp oil
1 tbsp finely
chopped dill
1 tbsp grated
Parmesan cheese
4 tbsp single cream

1 Cook the pasta in plenty of boiling salted water, according to the instructions on the packet, until al dente. Five minutes before the end of the cooking time, add the broccoli and cook with the pasta. Drain the pasta and broccoli in a sieve.

2 Rinse the salmon fillet in cold water, pat dry with kitchen paper, and chop into small pieces. Heat the oil in a frying pan and sauté the salmon pieces on all sides over a high heat. Season with salt.

3 Add the pasta, broccoli, dill, Parmesan, and cream to the salmon, and mix everything well. Let it simmer briefly until the sauce thickens. Season to taste with salt and pepper.

🕐  **ABOUT 20 MIN.**

🔪  **IN THE EVENING**

⬤  **WARM / COLD**

# COURGETTE CAMPANELLE
## WITH GOAT'S CHEESE AND THYME

Fresh thyme, mild goat's cheese, sautéed courgettes, and fine olive oil – these ingredients turn a simple pasta dish into an outstanding culinary experience. Whether you eat it warm or cold, this fragrant treat will bring comfort on even the most stressful of days.

## FOR 1 PERSON

100g (3½oz) campanelle
   or trompetti pasta
salt and pepper
½ courgette
2 tbsp olive oil
4 tbsp butter beans
   (tinned)
1 tbsp pine nuts, toasted
1 tsp chopped thyme
30g (1oz) soft goat's
   cheese

1 Cook the pasta in plenty of boiling salted water, according to the instructions on the packet, until al dente.

2 Meanwhile, cut the courgettes in half lengthways and slice thinly. Heat the olive oil in a pan and sauté the courgette slices for a few minutes until golden brown. Add the drained butter beans and cook briefly. Season with salt and pepper.

3 Drain the pasta and add to the vegetables, along with the pine nuts and thyme. Stir over the heat until warm, and season to taste with salt and pepper. Just before eating, crumble over the goat's cheese.

### QUICK ALTERNATIVES

Fancy some Asian-style spaghetti? Just leave out the feta, add a small handful of beansprouts, and season with soy or teriyaki sauce.

⏰ **ABOUT 15 MIN.**

✎ **IN THE EVENING**

◗ **WARM / COLD**

# CARROT SPELT SPAGHETTI
## WITH FETA AND SESAME

This unbelievably quick, wheat-free spaghetti recipe is a cross between a noodle salad and a pasta dish. Whether you eat it warm or cold, it always tastes wonderfully aromatic, thanks to the sweet carrots, sharp feta cheese, and nutty sesame. It's also very healthy: the perfect takeaway super food!

1 Cook the spaghetti in plenty of boiling salted water, according to the instructions on the packet, until al dente.

2 In the meantime, peel the carrots and slice into thin strips, using a potato peeler.

3 Drain the spaghetti in a sieve and return it to the saucepan. Stir the carrot strips, olive oil, salt, pepper, and most of the parsley into the warm spaghetti.

4 Sprinkle the spaghetti with the sesame seeds and remaining parsley, and crumble the feta on top.

## FOR 1 PERSON

100g (3½oz) spelt
  spaghetti
salt and pepper
1 carrot
2 tbsp olive oil
1 tbsp finely chopped
  parsley
2 tsp sesame seeds
40g (1½oz) feta cheese

# HERB ORECCHIETTE
## WITH TOASTED CAULIFLOWER, ALMONDS & PARMESAN

Toasted cauliflower is an unusual treat and eaten all too rarely. Combine it with orecchiette, fresh herbs, and almonds, and in no time you have a delicious pasta dish, which is also deceptively filling.

1 Cook the pasta in plenty of boiling salted water, according to the instructions on the packet, until al dente.

2 In the meantime, thinly slice the almonds. Heat 2 tbsp of olive oil in a pan and toast the cauliflower until golden brown. Add 100ml (3½fl oz) of water and let the cauliflower simmer until the water has evaporated.

3 Add the pasta, herbs, Parmesan, remaining olive oil, almonds, and pumpkin seeds to the cauliflower. Stir everything well and season with salt and pepper.

## FOR 1 PERSON

100g (3½oz) orecchiette
salt and pepper
6 almonds
3 tbsp olive oil
handful of cauliflower florets
1 tsp finely chopped thyme
1 tbsp finely chopped parsley
1 tbsp grated Parmesan cheese
1 tbsp pumpkin seeds

ABOUT 20 MIN.

IN THE EVENING

WARM / COLD

# MACARONI
## WITH PUMPKIN SEEDS,
## SPINACH PESTO & MOZZARELLA

---

## FOR 1 PERSON

100g (3½oz) macaroni
salt and pepper
handful of spinach leaves
2 tbsp olive oil
1 tbsp grated Parmesan
  cheese
2 tbsp pumpkin seeds
5 cherry tomatoes
4 mini mozzarella balls

Green spinach pesto made with nutty pumpkin seeds is a tasty, quick-to-prepare, vitamin-packed treat for your lunchbox. This green macaroni dish is delicious eaten warm, but you can also enjoy it as a cold pasta salad.

1 Cook the macaroni in plenty of boiling salted water, according to the instructions on the packet, until al dente.

2 Meanwhile, roughly chop the spinach. Put the spinach, olive oil, Parmesan, 1 tbsp pumpkin seeds, and a generous pinch of salt and pepper in a tall container and blend until smooth with a hand-held blender. Cut the cherry tomatoes and balls of mozzarella in half.

3 Drain the macaroni in a sieve and return it to the pan. Add the spinach pesto, tomatoes, mozzarella, and the remaining pumpkin seeds, and combine thoroughly. Season to taste with salt and pepper.

⏱ **ABOUT 20 MIN.**

🔪 **IN THE EVENING**

🎨 **WARM / COLD**

# SPAGHETTI
## WITH SPICY LENTIL BOLOGNAISE

Spaghetti with lentil bolognaise is a combination that tastes unbelievably delicious, is healthy, and super quick to prepare. Also, you don't have to go shopping specially – you'll find most of the ingredients in your kitchen cupboard.

## FOR 1 PERSON

100g (3½oz) spaghetti
salt and pepper
1 small onion
½ carrot
1 small chilli
1 tbsp olive oil
50g (1¾oz) red lentils
150g (5½oz) passata
 (from a jar)
1 spring onion
1 tbsp finely chopped
 coriander
1 tbsp Parmesan cheese
 shavings

1 Cook the spaghetti in plenty of boiling salted water, according to the instructions on the packet, until al dente.

2 In the meantime, peel and finely chop the onion and the carrot. Remove the stalk and seeds from the chilli and slice into fine rings.

3 Heat the olive oil in a pan and sauté the onion, carrot, chilli, and lentils for a few minutes. Add the passata and 100ml (3½fl oz) of water, and simmer everything over a low heat until the water has evaporated and the lentils are cooked.

4 Trim the root and green stem from the spring onion. Slice it into thin rings and stir into the lentil mixture, along with the coriander. Season the lentil bolognaise with salt and pepper. Drain the spaghetti and top with the lentil bolognaise. Before eating, scatter the Parmesan on top.

🕐 ABOUT 20 MIN.

🔪 IN THE EVENING

◖ WARM / COLD

## FOR 1 PERSON

100g (3½oz) conchiglie
   (pasta shells)
salt and pepper
120g (4½oz) pumpkin or
   squash, such as Red
   Kuri or butternut
2 chard leaves
2 tbsp olive oil
1 tsp butter
1 tbsp chopped walnuts
1 tsp finely chopped
   thyme
1 tbsp Parmesan cheese
   shavings

# CHARD CONCHIGLIE
## WITH SQUASH, WALNUTS, AND THYME

This sumptuous combination of sautéed squash, thyme,
walnuts, and fresh chard tastes fabulous – and it's also a
real feast for the eyes.

1 Cook the pasta in plenty of boiling salted water, following the
instructions on the packet, until al dente.

2 In the meantime, peel the squash if necessary, and chop it into
small pieces. Slice the chard into thin strips. Heat the olive oil
in a pan and sauté the squash and chard for a few minutes,
stirring occasionally. Pour in 100ml (3½fl oz) of water and let
the vegetables simmer until the water has evaporated.

3 Drain the pasta in a sieve. Add the pasta, butter, walnuts, and
thyme, mix well, and season with salt and pepper. Sprinkle with
the Parmesan just before serving.

ABOUT 20 MIN.

IN THE EVENING

COLD

# LAYERED SALAD
## WITH COURGETTE, ROCKET, AND FETA

**FOR 1 PERSON**

80g (3oz) orzo pasta
salt and pepper
handful of rocket
1 tomato
½ courgette
1 tbsp olive oil
1 tsp green pesto
50g (1¾oz) feta cheese

This pasta salad tastes of pure summer – whether you're eating it on a hot August day or in the depths of winter. Rocket, tomato, and feta add a Mediterranean flair, and it takes hardly any time to put together. While it's quite filling, it still tastes nice and light.

1 Cook the pasta in plenty of boiling salted water, according to the instructions on the packet, until al dente.

2 In the meantime, roughly chop the rocket. Halve the tomato, removing the core and seeds, then chop into small cubes. Finely dice the courgette and mix in a bowl with the tomato, olive oil, salt, and pepper.

3 Drain the pasta in a sieve. Transfer to a bowl and stir in the pesto and a pinch of salt and pepper. Put the pasta in a preserving jar and add the vegetables on top. Crumble over the feta cheese and, finally, place the rocket on top.

### TRANSPORT TIP
The layered salad looks fabulous in a preserving jar, but you can transport it in a plastic container just as easily.

# SAVOURY BREADS & PASTRIES

If you have a long daily commute, and not much time for cooking, home-made savoury breads and pastries are an excellent idea. You can make these recipes in minutes the night before, and they will still taste good the next day, whether eaten cold or heated up in the oven or microwave. Another advantage is that you can stash lots of vegetables in little quiches, empanadas, or samosas, which makes them super healthy, as well as super tasty. Breads and pastries are also easy to transport and not messy to eat – perfect if you're feeling peckish at your desk or even on the train home.

EACH ABOUT 15 MIN.

IN THE EVENING

WARM / COLD

# QUICHE LORRAINE TARTLETS

## FOR 4 TARTLETS

4 tbsp diced bacon
3 eggs
150g (5½oz) crème
  fraîche
150ml (5fl oz) milk
100g (3½oz) grated
  Gruyère cheese
2 tbsp finely chopped
  parsley
salt and pepper
butter for greasing
1 packet shortcrust
  pastry, about 270g
  (9½oz), chilled

1 Preheat the oven to 180°C (350°F/Gas 4). Fry the bacon in a pan without any fat for a few minutes, then put in a bowl. Add the eggs, crème fraîche, milk, cheese, parsley, and a generous pinch of salt and pepper. Beat everything together with a fork.

2 Grease four 12cm (5in) tartlet tins with a little butter. Divide the shortcrust pastry into four pieces, line the tartlet tins, and trim the overhanging edges. Prick the bases a few times with a fork and distribute the filling between the cases. Bake the tartlets on the middle shelf of the oven for about 20 minutes, until golden brown.

# PEPPER TARTLETS
## WITH GORGONZOLA

## FOR 4 TARTLETS

2 peppers
2 tbsp olive oil
3 eggs
150g (5½oz) crème fraîche
150ml (5fl oz) milk
1 tbsp finely chopped parsley
1 tbsp finely chopped thyme
salt and pepper
butter for greasing
1 packet shortcrust pastry,
  about 270g (9½oz), chilled
100g (3½oz) Gorgonzola
  cheese

1 Preheat the oven to 180°C (350°F/Gas 4). Halve the peppers, removing the stalks and seeds. Slice the peppers into thin strips. Heat the olive oil in a pan and sauté the pepper strips for a few minutes. Thoroughly whisk the eggs, crème fraîche, milk, parsley, thyme, and a generous pinch of salt and pepper in a bowl. Stir in the pepper pieces.

2 Grease four 12cm (5in) tartlet tins with a little butter. Divide the shortcrust pastry into four pieces, line the tartlet tins, and trim the overhanging edges. Prick the bases a few times with a fork, and distribute the filling equally between the cases. Chop the Gorgonzola into small pieces and scatter over the filling. Bake the tartlets on the middle shelf of the oven for around 20 minutes, until golden brown.

**TASTY TOGETHER**
These tartlets taste great on their own, but combined with a colourful salad, they make a fantastic lunch.

🕐 **ABOUT 30 MIN.**

✎ **IN THE EVENING**

◖ **WARM / COLD**

# INDIAN VEGETABLE SAMOSAS
## WITH CUCUMBER AND CORIANDER DIP

## FOR 8 SAMOSAS

1 carrot
1 potato
1 onion
1 pepper
1 tbsp oil
handful of frozen peas,
   defrosted
1 tbsp tomato purée
½ tsp curry powder
salt and pepper
1 packet filo pastry
   (4 sheets), about
   120g (4½oz), chilled
2 tbsp melted butter

## FOR THE DIP

½ cucumber
1 tbsp finely
   chopped
   coriander
200g (7oz) quark
   or curd cheese
salt and pepper

1 Preheat the oven to 180°C (350°F/Gas 4). Peel and finely dice the carrot, potato, and onion. Halve the pepper, remove the stalk and seeds, and chop finely. Heat the oil in a pan and sauté the carrot, potato, onion, and pepper for a few minutes. Add the peas, tomato purée, and curry powder, and continue to sauté. Season with salt and pepper.

2 Lay out two sheets of filo pastry, brush with a little butter, and cover with the two remaining pastry sheets. Cut these two doubled filo sheets into four strips. Spoon 1 tbsp of the vegetable filling onto the lower end of each strip of pastry. Fold the right lower edge up to the left, and the left lower edge up to the right. Repeat this process until the whole pastry strip has been folded together.

3 Lay the triangles on a baking tray lined with greaseproof paper and brush with the remaining butter. Bake the samosas on the middle shelf of the oven for about 15 minutes, until golden brown.

4 Meanwhile, for the dip, coarsely grate the cucumber and combine with the coriander and quark in a bowl. Season well with salt and pepper. Serve the dip with the samosas.

EACH ABOUT 15 MIN.

IN THE EVENING

WARM / COLD

# PIZZA POCKETS

Pizza dough pockets are quick to make, and refreshingly varied, because you can fill them with so many different types of ingredients. They taste great fresh from the oven, but just as good cold or reheated the next day. They're simply a brilliant quick snack that you can take anywhere.

## FOR 4 PIZZA POCKETS

1 aubergine
2 tbsp olive oil
150g (5½oz) ricotta cheese
2 tbsp finely chopped
  thyme
salt and pepper
1 packet pizza dough,
  about 400g (14oz), chilled

# AUBERGINE RICOTTA POCKETS
## WITH THYME

1 Preheat the oven to 180°C (350°F/Gas 4). Line a baking tray with greaseproof paper.

2 Cut the aubergine lengthways into slices and then into cubes. Heat the olive oil in a pan and sauté the aubergine cubes until golden brown. Stir in the ricotta and thyme and season the mixture with salt and pepper.

3 Cut the pizza dough into four and place a quarter of the filling in the middle of each rectangle. Brush the edges with a little water, fold the dough over, and round the corners with a knife to form a semi-circle. Press the edges firmly together.

4 Lay the pizza pockets on the baking tray and bake on the middle shelf of the oven for about 20 minutes, until golden brown.

## TRY IT THIS WAY TOO
As an alternative to aubergine, try filling the pockets with courgette, pepper, or roasted squash.

# FETA POCKETS
## WITH TOMATOES, OLIVES, AND CHILLIES

These pizza pockets are the culinary equivalent of a Greek summer. With salty feta and juicy tomatoes, aromatic oregano and chilli, all wrapped up in crispy dough, they can keep you going through the greyest of days

1 Preheat the oven to 180°C (350°F/Gas 4). Line a baking tray with greaseproof paper.

2 Crumble the feta into a bowl and add the Emmental. Finely chop the olives and chilli peppers. Halve the tomato, removing the core and seeds, and dice the flesh. Add the olives and chillies, tomato, parsley, oregano, and olive oil to the cheese and combine everything thoroughly.

3 Cut the pizza dough into four pieces and place a quarter of the filling in the middle of each rectangle. Brush the edges with a little water, fold the pockets together, and trim the corners off with a knife to form a semi-circle. Press the edges of the dough firmly together.

4 Lay the pizza pockets on the baking tray and bake on the middle shelf of the oven for about 20 minutes, until golden brown.

## FOR 4
## PIZZA POCKETS

150g (5½oz) feta cheese
50g (1¾oz) grated
  Emmental cheese
8 olives, pitted
6 pickled chilli peppers
  (from a jar)
1 tomato
1 tbsp finely chopped
  parsley
1 tsp dried oregano
2 tbsp olive oil
1 packet pizza dough,
  about 400g (14oz),
  chilled

# LEEK EMPANADAS
## WITH RICE

---

### FOR 8 EMPANADAS

1 small leek
2 tbsp olive oil
50g (1¾oz) long-grain
    rice
salt and pepper
2 tbsp finely
    chopped dill
1 packet pizza
    dough, about 400g
    (14oz), chilled
1 egg yolk

1 Preheat the oven to 180°C (350°F/Gas 4). Line a baking tray with greaseproof paper.

2 Remove the root and outer leaves of the leek. Cut the leek in half lengthways, wash thoroughly, and slice into thin rings. Heat the olive oil in the pan and fry the leek for a few minutes until softened. Add the rice, sauté briefly, then pour in 200ml (7fl oz) of water. Let the rice simmer until the water has evaporated. Season with salt and pepper, and stir in the dill. Set aside to cool.

3 Cut out sixteen 5cm (2in) circles from the pizza dough, using a cookie cutter or cup. Divide the leek filling among half of the dough circles, placing it in the centre of each one. Brush the edges with a little water. Place the remaining dough circles on top. Press the edges of the dough pockets firmly together all around, using a fork. With a sharp knife, make three small holes in the top of each one.

4 Place the dough pockets on the baking tray and brush with the egg yolk. Bake the empanadas on the middle shelf of the oven for about 15 minutes, until golden brown.

LEEK EMPANADAS

# CHEESE AND SPINACH EMPANADAS
## WITH CARAWAY SEEDS

### FOR 8 EMPANADAS

1 onion
200g (7oz) spinach
1 tbsp olive oil
80g (3oz) grated
   Gruyère cheese
salt and pepper
1 packet pizza dough,
   about 400g (14oz),
   chilled
1 egg yolk
2 tbsp caraway seeds

1 Preheat the oven to 180°C (350°F/Gas 4). Line a baking tray with greaseproof paper.

2 Peel and dice the onion. Roughly chop the spinach. Heat the olive oil in a pan and sauté the onion. Add the spinach and continue to cook briefly until it wilts. Stir in the cheese and season with salt and pepper. Set aside to cool.

3 Cut out sixteen 5cm (2in) circles from the pizza dough, using a cookie cutter or cup. Divide the spinach filling among half of the dough circles, placing it in the centre of each one. Brush the edges with a little water. Place the remaining dough circles on top. Press the edges of the dough pockets firmly together all around, using a fork. With a sharp knife, make three small holes in the top of each one.

4 Place the dough pockets on the baking tray and brush with the egg yolk. Sprinkle with the caraway seeds. Bake the empanadas on the middle shelf of the oven for about 15 minutes, until golden brown.

Pumpkin
Muffins

Courgette
Pumpkin
Seed muffins

# PUMPKIN MUFFINS
## WITH FETA, PECANS, AND THYME

### FOR 6 MUFFINS

butter for greasing
150g (5½oz) pumpkin or
   squash, such as Red
   Kuri or butternut
200g (7oz) plain flour
2 tsp baking powder
60ml (2fl oz) olive oil
250ml (9fl oz) milk
80g (3oz) quark or curd
   cheese
1 egg
3 tbsp roughly chopped
   pecans
salt and pepper
120g (4½oz) feta cheese
2 tbsp finely chopped
   thyme

1 Preheat the oven to 180°C (350°F/Gas 4). Grease six of the
  moulds in a muffin tray with a little butter.

2 Peel the squash if necessary, and coarsely grate the flesh. Put
  the squash and other ingredients (except the feta and thyme)
  in a bowl and combine with a hand-held blender until smooth.

3 Divide the mixture among the muffin moulds, and scatter with
  the crumbled feta and thyme. Bake the muffins on the middle
  oven shelf for about 20 minutes, until golden brown.

# COURGETTE
# PUMPKIN SEED MUFFINS

### FOR 6 MUFFINS

butter for greasing
1 small courgette
5 tbsp pumpkin seeds
1 egg
200g (7oz) plain flour
2 tsp baking powder
100ml (3½fl oz) milk
55ml (2fl oz) olive oil
80g (3oz) quark or curd
   cheese
3 tbsp grated Parmesan
   cheese
salt and pepper

1 Preheat the oven to 180°C (350°F/Gas 4). Grease six of the
  moulds in a muffin tray with a little butter.

2 Coarsely grate the courgette into a bowl and lightly squeeze
  out any moisture with your hands. Finely chop half the pumpkin
  seeds, and add to the bowl with the rest of the pumpkin seeds.
  Add the egg, flour, baking powder, milk, olive oil, quark or curd
  cheese, Parmesan, and a generous pinch of salt and pepper.
  Beat with a hand-held blender until smooth.

3 Divide the mixture among the six muffin moulds. Bake
  the muffins on the middle shelf of the oven for about
  20 minutes, until golden brown.

⏰ **ABOUT 20 MIN.**

🔪 **IN THE EVENING**

🌡 **WARM / COLD**

# OLIVE PLAITS
## WITH FETA CREAM

## FOR 2 OLIVE PLAITS

**small handful of green
olives, pitted**
**1 tbsp finely chopped
rosemary**
**1 packet pizza dough,
about 400g (14oz),
chilled**
**1 tbsp olive oil**
**1 tsp dried oregano**

## FOR THE FETA CREAM

**80g (3oz) feta cheese**
**3 tbsp natural yogurt**
**2 tbsp olive oil**
**1 tsp finely chopped
parsley**
**1 tsp dried oregano**
**pepper**

Baking bread doesn't have to be something you can only do at weekends. With this handy cheat – ready-made pizza dough from the fridge – you can put delicious-smelling bread on the table in no time at all. Pep up the dough with fresh herbs and olives to make it even more special.

1   Preheat the oven to 180°C (350°F/Gas 4). Line a baking tray with greaseproof paper. Chop the olives finely and mix with the rosemary.

2   Cut the pizza dough lengthways into six strips of equal width. Use three strips to make each plait, adding the olive rosemary mixture as you go. This works best if you place a little filling onto the dough before you fold it over. Lay the plaits on the baking tray, brush with the olive oil, and sprinkle with oregano. Bake on the middle shelf of the oven for about 15 minutes, until golden brown.

3   Meanwhile, to make the feta cream, crumble the feta into a bowl. Add the yogurt, olive oil, parsley, oregano, and a generous pinch of pepper, and mix everything together to make a smooth cream. Serve the feta cream with the olive plaits, while they're still slightly warm.

**TRANSPORT TIP**
Store the feta cream in a small plastic box ready for lunch. Simply wrap the cooled olive plaits in a sheet of foil.

ABOUT 20 MIN.

IN THE EVENING

WARM / COLD

## FOR 6 PUMPKIN ROLLS

600g (1lb 5oz) pumpkin
   or squash, such as Red
   Kuri or butternut
1 onion
3 tbsp rosemary
3 tbsp butter
2 tbsp raisins
4 tbsp flaked almonds
salt and pepper
1 packet filo pastry
   (4 sheets), about 120g
   (4½oz), chilled

# PUMPKIN ROLLS
## WITH ROSEMARY AND ALMONDS

These pumpkin rolls are really little pastries, inspired by the
Turkish börek, which is made from filo pastry and filled with
feta cheese, spinach, or minced meat. Inside they're super
juicy, but deliciously crisp on the outside – just like these
pumpkin rolls. The almonds and aromatic rosemary give
the filling a more complex flavour and a bit of bite.

1 Peel the squash if necessary and coarsely grate the flesh.
   Peel and finely dice the onion. Roughly chop the rosemary.
   Heat 1 tbsp butter in a pan and sauté the onion and squash
   for a few minutes, until the squash is soft and golden brown.
   Stir in the raisins and half of the flaked almonds. Season with
   salt and pepper, and let the mixture cool down slightly.
   Preheat the oven to 180°C (350°F/Gas 4). Line a baking tray
   with greaseproof paper.

2 In the meantime, melt the remaining butter. Lay out two
   sheets of filo pastry, brush with a little butter, and cover with
   the two remaining pastry sheets. Cut these two doubled filo
   sheets into six equal rectangles. Place the filling on the
   lower long edge of each rectangle, fold the sides in over
   the filling, and roll up the strudel from this lower end.
   Lay the pumpkin rolls seam down on the baking tray.

3 Brush the pumpkin rolls with the remaining butter and sprinkle
   with the rest of the almonds and the rosemary. Then bake on
   the middle shelf of the oven for about 15 minutes, until
   golden brown.

## GOES WELL WITH

Freshly baked, warm bread rolls taste divine with aromatic soft cheese, or even just with butter. Pep up the pide with a crunchy salad, sliced tomato, and a dollop of soured cream.

EACH ABOUT 15 MIN.

IN THE EVENING

WARM / COLD

## PIZZA DOUGH

Ready-made pizza dough is an ingenious all-rounder. It lets you bake irresistible delicacies in the blink of an eye, and is delicious topped with vegetables, cheese, bacon, or minced meat. It's also really easy to bake bread and rolls from this light dough.

# WALNUT RICOTTA BREAD ROLLS
## WITH THYME

## FOR 8 ROLLS

250g (9oz) ricotta cheese

5 tbsp finely chopped walnuts

4 tbsp finely chopped thyme

salt and pepper

1 packet pizza dough, about 400g (14oz), chilled

Inspired by the Italian combination of walnuts and ricotta, drizzled with honey and eaten as a dessert, these little pizza-dough bread rolls are luscious and piquant.

1 Preheat the oven to 180°C (350°F/Gas 4). Line a baking tray with greaseproof paper. Put the ricotta, 4 tbsp of walnuts and 3 tbsp of thyme into a bowl and season with a generous pinch of salt and pepper.

2 Divide the pizza dough into eight equal squares, and distribute the ricotta filling between them, placing it in the centre of each square. Press the dough firmly over the filling and shape into round rolls.

3 Place the rolls seam down on the baking tray. Scatter with the remaining walnuts and thyme and press down gently. Bake the rolls on the middle oven shelf for about 15 minutes, until golden brown.

# MINCED MEAT PIDE
## WITH CORIANDER & PINE NUTS

This is a recreation of the traditional Turkish meat pide. It is really easy to make and, when you know what's in it, tastes even better!

1 Preheat the oven to 180°C (350°F/Gas 4). Line a baking tray with greaseproof paper. Peel and dice the onion. Remove the stalk and seeds from the chilli and chop it finely. Heat the olive oil in a pan and sauté the onion, chilli, beef, and tomato purée until the meat juices have evaporated. Stir in the coriander and pine nuts, and season with salt and pepper.

2 Cut a large oval from the pizza dough, lay it on the baking tray, and fold over the edges slightly (see photo on p128). Spread the meat mixture over it. Bake the pide on the middle shelf of the oven for about 15 minutes, until golden brown.

## FOR 1 PERSON

1 small onion
½ chilli
2 tbsp olive oil
150g (5½oz) minced beef
1 tsp tomato purée
2 tbsp finely chopped coriander
2 tbsp pine nuts, toasted
salt and pepper
½ packet pizza dough, about 200g (7oz), chilled

# POTATO MINI PIZZA
## WITH GOAT'S CHEESE AND ROSEMARY

1 Preheat the oven to 180°C (350°F/Gas 4). Line a baking tray with greaseproof paper. Peel the potatoes and slice thinly using a potato peeler. Cut six 5cm (2in) circles from the pizza dough, using a cookie cutter, small bowl, or cup, and lay them on the baking tray.

2 Smear the dough circles with the goat's cheese and lay overlapping potato slices on top. Season with salt and pepper and sprinkle with rosemary. Bake the mini pizzas on the middle shelf of the oven for about 12 minutes, until golden brown.

## FOR 6 MINI PIZZAS

3 potatoes
1 packet pizza dough, about 400g (14oz), chilled
150g (5½oz) soft goat's cheese
salt and pepper
4 tbsp rosemary

## GOURMET TIP

No one can resist
oven-warm scones with
a slice of melting butter.
A heavenly treat!

# CLASSIC SCONES
## WITH CARROT SUGAR NUT BUTTER

### FOR ABOUT 10 SCONES

200g (7oz) plain flour,
    plus extra for dusting
1 tsp baking powder
80g (3oz) butter
100ml (3½fl oz) milk
1 tsp salt

### FOR THE BUTTER

½ carrot
60g (2oz) butter,
    softened
1 tbsp demerara sugar
1 tbsp finely chopped
    hazelnuts

### FOR ABOUT 10 SCONES

200g (7oz) white spelt
    flour, plus extra for
    dusting
1 tsp baking powder
80g (3oz) butter
100ml (3½fl oz) milk
2 tbsp finely chopped
    herbs, such as thyme,
    rosemary, and parsley
60g (2oz) grated
    Gruyère cheese
1 tsp salt

1 Preheat the oven to 180°C (350°F/Gas 4). Line a baking tray with greaseproof paper. For the scones, put all the ingredients into a bowl and combine with your hands, kneading the mixture into a dough.

2 Roll out the dough on a floured work surface to about 1cm (½in) thickness, and use a glass to cut out about ten 4cm (2in) scones. Lay them on the baking tray. Bake the scones on the middle shelf of the oven for about 15 minutes, until golden brown.

3 For the butter, peel the carrot, grate it finely, and lightly squeeze out any excess moisture. Mix the carrot, butter, sugar, and nuts in a bowl with a fork.

# HERBY CHEESE SCONES
## WITH SPELT FLOUR

Robust spelt flour makes these scones extra hearty and filling, while the tangy cheese and fresh herbs smell amazing. Before baking, try topping the scones with a little extra cheese.

1 Preheat the oven to 180°C (350°F/Gas 4). Line a baking tray with greaseproof paper. Put all the ingredients into a bowl and knead to a firm dough with your hands.

2 Roll out the dough on a floured work surface to about 1cm (½in) thickness, and use a glass to cut out about ten 4cm (2in) scones. Lay them on the baking tray. Bake the scones on the middle oven shelf for about 15 minutes, until golden brown.

# SWEET THINGS

There's nothing like a sweet treat to get you in a good mood fast, as well as topping up your energy levels. And it feels even better if you can find a moment of calm amidst the day's hustle and bustle in which to eat it. This chapter contains an assortment of sweet life-savers that taste brilliant, are quick to prepare, and above all easy to transport. Whether it's super healthy energy bars with nuts and dried fruits, tastily filled muffins, or crispy pains au chocolat that make your mouth water, there's something here for everyone.

⏱ ABOUT 15 MIN.

✎ IN THE EVENING

◗ COLD

# MUESLI BARS
## WITH DRIED FRUITS, SESAME SEEDS & NUTS

---

## FOR ABOUT 10 BARS

5 dried apricots

3 tbsp dried cranberries

40g (1¼oz) butter, plus extra for greasing

120g (4½oz) runny honey

150g (5½oz) jumbo oats

2 tbsp desiccated coconut

2 tbsp sesame seeds

3 tbsp chopped almonds

3 tbsp chopped hazelnuts

Making muesli bars yourself is child's play and super quick. But the best thing about making your own is that you can choose exactly what goes into them. The ingredients for these sugar-free bars of energy include various crunchy nuts, dried fruits, and honey. Simple, healthy, and delicious!

1 Preheat the oven to 180°C (350°F/Gas 4). Finely chop the apricots and cranberries. Melt the butter and honey in a small saucepan and mix with the other ingredients in a bowl.

2 Tip the mixture into a greased, rectangular 20×28cm (8 x 11in) baking tin, and press down firmly with your hands.

3 Bake the muesli mixture on the middle shelf for about 15–20 minutes until golden brown and firm to the touch. While it is still warm, cut into about ten bars, and leave to cool.

## STORAGE TIP
Store the muesli bars in a well-sealed tin to keep them nice and crunchy.

🕐 EACH ABOUT 15 MIN.

🔪 IN THE EVENING

🔵 COLD

# NUT COOKIES
## WITH RAISINS

### FOR 6 COOKIES

**50g (1¾oz) plain flour**
**125g (4½oz) oats**
**½ tsp baking powder**
**1 pinch salt**
**100g (3½oz) brown sugar**
**100g (3½oz) butter**
**1 egg yolk**
**2 tbsp raisins**
**3 tbsp mixed chopped nuts, such as almonds and hazelnuts**

1  Preheat the oven to 180°C (350°F/Gas 4). Line a baking tray with greaseproof paper. Put all the ingredients in a bowl, combine with your hands, and knead to a firm dough.

2  Divide the dough and roll into six equal balls, place them well spaced apart on the baking tray, and press flat into circles. Bake the cookies on the middle oven shelf for about 15 minutes, until golden brown.

# CRAZY OREO COOKIES
## WITH M&M'S

### FOR 6 COOKIES

**50g (1¾oz) plain flour**
**125g (4½oz) oats**
**½ tsp baking powder**
**1 pinch salt**
**100g (3½oz) sugar**
**100g (3½oz) butter**
**1 egg yolk**
**3 Oreo cookies**
**24 M&M's**

1  Preheat the oven to 180°C (350°F/Gas 4). Line a baking tray with greaseproof paper. Put all the ingredients except the cookies and sweets into a bowl, and combine with your hands to form a firm dough.

2  Divide the dough and roll into six equal balls, place them well spaced apart on the baking tray, and press flat into circles. Break the cookies into small pieces and press them into the dough. Likewise, distribute the M&M's among the cookies and press them in slightly. Bake the cookies on the middle oven shelf for about 15 minutes, until golden brown.

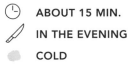

🕐 **ABOUT 15 MIN.**

🔪 **IN THE EVENING**

🔵 **COLD**

Admittedly this recipe isn't faithful to the traditional, buttery Scottish biscuits that crumble delicately in the mouth. But the end result is just as crumbly and delicious. Sandwiched between crisp pastry and a crumble topping is a tart blueberry filling, making these bars the perfect sweet snack for travelling

# BLUEBERRY SHORTBREAD BARS

## FOR ABOUT 10 PIECES

**200g (7oz) sugar**
**1 egg**
**220g (8oz) butter, plus**
  **extra for greasing**
**350g (12oz) plain flour**
**1 tsp baking powder**
**1 pinch salt**
**grated zest of 1 lemon**
**150g (5½oz) blueberry jam**

1 Preheat the oven to 180°C (350°F/Gas 4). Grease a 20 x 28cm (8 x 11in) baking tin with a little butter.

2 Put the sugar, egg, butter, flour, baking powder, salt, and lemon zest into a bowl, and combine with your hands into a light, crumbly dough.

3 Place about three-quarters of the dough into the tin and press down to form a firm base. Spread the jam on top of this and then crumble the remaining dough over the top.

4 Bake on the middle oven shelf for about 35 minutes, until golden brown. After 25 minutes, cover the tin with foil, so that the crumble topping doesn't get too brown.

5 Let the blueberry shortbread cool in the tin, then cut into about 10 bars.

# CLASSIC ROLLS

**FOR 12 ROLLS**

about 20g fresh yeast
500g (1lb 2oz) plain
  flour
100g (3½oz) sugar
butter for greasing

1 Dissolve the yeast by stirring it into 300ml (10fl oz) of lukewarm water. Put the flour and sugar in a bowl, add the yeast and water, and knead to a firm dough, using the dough hook of a hand-held blender.

2 Cover the bowl with a tea towel, and leave the dough to prove in a warm place for about 30 minutes.

3 Preheat the oven to 180°C (350°F/Gas 4). Grease a 12-mould muffin tray with butter. Divide the dough into 12 equal balls and place them in the muffin tray. Bake on the middle oven shelf for about 20 minutes, until golden brown.

# CHOCO ROLLS

**FOR 12 ROLLS**

about 20g fresh yeast
500g (1lb 2oz) plain
  flour
100g (3½oz) sugar
butter for greasing
4 tbsp finely chopped
  dark chocolate

1 Dissolve the yeast by stirring it into 300ml (10fl oz) of lukewarm water. Put the flour and sugar in a bowl, add the yeast and water, and knead to a firm dough, using the dough hook of a hand-held blender. Cover the bowl with a tea towel, and leave the dough to prove in a warm place for about 30 minutes.

2 Preheat the oven to 180°C (350°F/Gas 4). Grease a 12-mould muffin tray with butter. Knead the chocolate into the dough. Divide the dough into 12 equal balls and place them in the muffin tray. Bake on the middle oven shelf for about 20 minutes, until golden brown.

EACH ABOUT 15 MIN.

IN THE EVENING

WARM / COLD

## PARISIAN DELICACIES

# PETITS PAINS
## AU CHOCOLAT

**FOR 6 PETITS PAINS**

1 packet croissant
dough, about 340g
(12oz), chilled
12 narrow pieces
of dark chocolate
1 egg yolk

1 Preheat the oven to 180°C (350°F/Gas 4). Line a baking tray with greaseproof paper.

2 Cut the dough into six rectangles, each measuring about 8 x 12cm (3 x 5in). Place a piece of chocolate on each of the short edges, then roll up both of these ends towards the middle of the dough. Place the petits pains onto the baking tray, open side down, and brush with the egg yolk. Bake the petits pains on the middle oven shelf for about 15 minutes, until golden brown.

# MARZIPAN AND NUT
# CROISSANTS

**FOR 6 CROISSANTS**

4 tbsp ground
hazelnuts
1 tbsp melted butter
1 tbsp sugar
4 tbsp marzipan,
grated
2 tbsp cinnamon
sugar
1 packet croissant
dough, about 340g
(12oz), chilled

1 Preheat the oven to 180°C (350°F/Gas 4). Line a baking tray with greaseproof paper.

2 Mix the hazelnuts, butter, sugar, and marzipan in a bowl. Sprinkle the cinnamon sugar over a plate.

3 Following the instructions on the packet, cut six croissant triangles out of the dough. Spread the marzipan nut mixture equally over the widest side of the triangles, and roll the croissants up from this edge. Roll the croissants in the cinnamon sugar, place on the baking tray, and bake on the middle oven shelf for around 15 minutes, until golden brown.

zen oder
chen Fettstoffen

e Braten so viel als
r Saft und Fett anzu-
, um ein übermäßiges
nen Fleisches zu ver-
stoff wird, wenn auch
haften. Geschmack
reich gibt es viele brat-
liche Magerkeit, oder auch
die andere Wirkung des
dlichen, bis heute? Falle

dienst anstelle der anderthalb Jahre Militärdienst entschie-
den, als Museumswächter einzusetzen. Der Vorschlag war
nicht einmal bis in den Sitzungssaal des Senats gekommen.

Angenommen, Semenzato hatte bei der Unterschiebung
von Fälschungen die Hand im Spiel, über wen ließen sich
die Originale dann besser an den Mann bringen als über
einen Antiquitätenhändler? Der hätte nicht nur die Kund-
schaft und die Sachkenntnis, um den Wert zutreffend zu
schätzen, er würde auch wissen, wie man sie unbehelligt
von Polizei, Guardia di Finanza oder Kulturgüterkom-
mission veräußerte. Es war ein Kinderspiel, Kunstschätze
ins Land oder außer Landes zu bringen. Ein Blick auf die
Landkarte Italiens zeigte, wie durchlässig die Grenzen
waren. Tausende Kilometer verschwiegener Buchten, ein-
samer Meeresarme und abgelegener Strände. Und für die-
jenigen, die gut organisiert waren oder gute Beziehungen
hatten, gab es die See- und Flughäfen, über die man unge-
straft alles schleusen konnte. Nicht nur Museumswächter
waren schlecht bezahlt.

Brunettis Tagträumerei wurde durch ein Klopfen an der
Tür unterbrochen. »Avanti«, rief er und machte das Fen-
ster zu. Wieder Zeit zum Schmoren.

Signorina Elettra kam ins Zimmer, in der einen Hand
einen Notizblock, in der anderen eine Akte. »Ich habe den
Namen des Capitano gefunden, Commissario. Carrara
heißt er, Giulio Carrara. Er ist noch in Rom, wurde aber
letztes Jahr zum maggiore befördert.«

»Wie haben Sie das herausbekommen, Signorina?«

»Ich habe bei seiner Dienststelle in Rom angerufen und
mit seiner Sekretärin gesprochen. Ich habe ihm ausrichten

173

⏱ EACH ABOUT 10 MIN.

🔪 IN THE EVENING

🌓 WARM / COLD

## WAFFLES

Waffles are quick to make and you can eat them on their own, or with cream, yogurt, or a fruit compote. Delicious eaten straight out of the waffle maker, they are just as tasty when cold, making them the perfect little take-away sweet for when you're travelling or at the office.

# HONEY NUT WAFFLES
## WITH SPELT AND CINNAMON

### FOR 2 WAFFLES

1 egg
60ml (2fl oz) milk
1 tbsp brown sugar
1 tbsp honey
90g (3oz) spelt flour
½ tsp baking powder
½ tsp ground cinnamon
40g (1½oz) melted butter
2 tbsp finely chopped nuts,
   such as walnuts, almonds

1 Place the egg, milk, sugar, honey, flour, baking powder, cinnamon, about three-quarters of the butter, and the nuts in a bowl. Whisk together, using a balloon whisk, to form a smooth batter.

2 Heat the waffle maker and brush with some of the remaining butter. Pour in half the batter, close the lid, and cook the waffle for about 5 minutes, until golden brown. Remove the waffle, and cook the second half of the batter in the same way.

# BLUEBERRY COCONUT WAFFLES

### FOR 2 WAFFLES

1 egg
60ml (2fl oz) milk
3 tbsp sugar
90g (3oz) plain flour
½ tsp baking powder
40g (1½oz) butter
2 tbsp desiccated coconut
small handful of blueberries

1 Place the egg, milk, sugar, flour, baking powder, around three-quarters of the butter, and the desiccated coconut in a bowl. Whisk together, using a balloon whisk, to form a smooth batter. Fold in the blueberries.

2 Heat the waffle maker and brush with some of the remaining butter. Pour in half the batter, close the lid, and cook the waffle for about 5 minutes, until golden brown. Remove the waffle, and cook the second half of the batter in the same way.

Very Berry
Lemon Muffins

**Muesli Banana Muffins**

**Peanut Butter and Jelly Muffins**

🕐  EACH ABOUT 15 MIN.

🔪  IN THE EVENING

☁  COLD

FILLED MUFFINS

# VERY BERRY LEMON MUFFINS

## FOR 8 MUFFINS

80g (3oz) butter, plus
   extra for greasing
100g (3½oz) sugar
1 egg
250g (9oz) plain flour
90ml (3fl oz) milk
2 tsp baking powder
handful of berries
6 tsp lemon curd or
   lemon marmalade

1 Preheat the oven to 180°C (350°F/Gas 4). Grease eight of the moulds in a muffin tray with some butter. Beat the softened butter with the sugar and egg in a bowl, using a hand whisk, until light and fluffy. Add the flour, milk, and baking powder, and mix until smooth. Fold in the berries with a spoon.

2 Distribute half the mixture among the moulds and put 1 tsp lemon curd or marmalade on top of each. Cover with the remaining mixture and bake the muffins on the middle oven shelf for about 25 minutes, until golden brown.

# MUESLI BANANA MUFFINS
## WITH CHOCOLATE

## FOR 8 MUFFINS

80g (3oz) butter, plus
   extra for greasing
100g (3½oz) sugar
1 egg
250g (9oz) plain flour
90ml (3fl oz) milk
2 tsp baking powder
4 tbsp muesli
1 banana
8 tsp chocolate
   hazelnut spread

1 Preheat the oven to 180°C (350°F/Gas 4). Grease eight of the moulds in a muffin tray with butter. Beat the softened butter with the sugar and egg in a bowl, using a hand whisk, until light and fluffy. Add the flour, milk, baking powder, and muesli, and mix until smooth. Peel the banana and slice thinly.

2 Distribute half the mixture among the moulds and put 1 tsp chocolate spread on top of each. Cover with the remaining mixture and top with banana slices. Bake the muffins on the middle oven shelf for about 25 minutes, until golden brown.

# PEANUT BUTTER AND JELLY MUFFINS
## WITH CRUNCHY NUT TOPPING

## FOR 8 MUFFINS

80g (3oz) butter, plus
 extra for greasing
100g (3½oz) sugar
1 egg
250g (9oz) plain flour
90ml (3fl oz) milk
2 tsp baking powder
2 tbsp peanut butter
8 tsp raspberry jam

## FOR THE TOPPING

1 tbsp butter
2 tbsp plain flour
1 tbsp sugar
1 tbsp ground hazelnuts

1 Preheat the oven to 180°C (350°F/Gas 4). Grease eight of the moulds in a muffin tray with butter. Beat the softened butter with the sugar and egg in a bowl, using a hand whisk, until light and fluffy. Add the flour, milk, baking powder, and peanut butter, and mix until smooth.

2 Distribute half the mixture among the moulds and put 1 tsp raspberry jam on top of each. Cover with the remaining mixture.

3 For the topping, rub the butter, flour, sugar, and hazelnuts together in a bowl to make crumbs. Sprinkle the crumble over the top of the muffins. Bake the muffins on the middle oven shelf for about 25 minutes, until golden brown.

# THE WEEKLY PLANNER
## RECIPE IDEAS FOR EVERY SITUATION

Sometimes, in the hustle and bustle of everyday life, making the effort to eat well feels just too hard. There are so many other things buzzing around in your head that food gets neglected. But it's important to reflect on your diet now and then, and to focus on high-quality seasonal ingredients – that's how you stay fit and in good spirits. All of which is achieved in no time with the crafty weekly planner and its five recipe ideas, suitable for breakfast, lunch, or dinner.

## LOVELY LUNCHES
# FOR EVERYDAY LIFE

### GO GREEN – FULL OF FRUIT AND VEG

**Day 1** Soft crunch start: Raspberry Muesli with Sesame and Pumpkin Seed Crunch **(see p23)**

**Day 2** Shake It Low: Strawberry Cheesecake Milkshake **(see p33)**

**Day 3** Full of vegetables and pulses: Carrot and Red Lentil Stew with Coconut **(see p88)**

**Day 4** Power into the afternoon: Bean and Spinach Stew **(see p87)**

**Day 5** Fluffy and flavourful: Pepper Tartlets with Gorgonzola **(see p114)**

### IN A JIFFY – SPEEDY STUFF FOR HECTIC DAYS

**Day 1** Stirred in 10 minutes: Blueberry and Almond Oatmeal **(see p20)**

**Day 2** Piled up in 20 minutes: Layered Salad with Courgette, Rocket, and Feta **(see p111)**

**Day 3** Folded in 10 minutes: Vegetable Quesadilla with Mozzarella **(see p53)**

**Day 4** Dressed in 15 minutes: A Kind of Waldorf Salad **(see p58)**

**Day 5** Plated up in 5 minutes: Chicken Ciabatta with Roquefort, Pumpkin Seeds, and Radicchio **(see p36)**

### LIVE LIGHT – FOR CALORIE COUNTERS

**Day 1** Mango Maple Muesli **(about 500kcal, see p23)**

**Day 2** Glass Noodle Salad with Green Beans, Roasted Chickpeas, Chilli, and Peanuts **(about 500kcal, see p75)**

**Day 3** Hot Bean Burrito with Avocado **(about 400kcal, see p48)**

**Day 4** Salad Like They Serve in Nice **(about 350kcal, see p58)**

**Day 5** Multicoloured Minestrone **(about 350kcal, see p92)**

## WITH RECIPES TO SUIT
# EVERY SEASON

### KEEP A COOL HEAD ON HOT DAYS

**Day 1** Cool breakfast – preferably enjoyed "on the rocks" with a couple of ice cubes: Avocado Yogurt Shake **(see p32)**

**Day 2** Nice and easy at lunchtime: Well chilled Tomato Bread Salad with Pesto and Pine Nuts **(see p64)**

**Day 3** Almost like on holiday: Greek Ciabatta Sandwich with Feta and Pine Nuts **(see p40)**

**Day 4** Indulgence hot or cold: Broccoli Bows with Sautéed Salmon and Dill **(see p97)**

**Day 5** Aromatically fruity speed bake: Blueberry Coconut Waffles **(see p147)**

### SPRINGTIME IN YOUR STOMACH

**Day 1** Fresh veg throughout the day: Grilled Cheese Sandwich with Courgette and Ricotta **(see p39)**

**Day 2** Longing for the south: Artichoke and Courgette Focaccia with Red Pesto and Mozzarella **(see p51)**

**Day 3** Like a breath of fresh air: Herb Orecchiette with Toasted Cauliflower, Almonds, and Parmesan **(see p102)**

**Day 4** Colourful lunch: Tofu Vegetable Ratatouille with Couscous **(see p82)**

**Day 5** Floral pasta: Courgette Campanelle with Goat's Cheese and Thyme **(see p98)**

### WARD OFF AUTUMNAL WOES

**Day 1** Happy days: Apple Strudel Rice Pudding with Almonds, Raisins, and Cinnamon **(see p24)**

**Day 2** Warm and comforting: Spaghetti with Spicy Lentil Bolognaise **(see p107)**

**Day 3** Warms stomach and soul: Carrot and Red Lentil Stew with Coconut **(see p88)**

**Day 4** Luncheon leaves: Apple Walnut Bread with Brie and Cranberries **(see p38)**

**Day 5** Crumbly delights: Blueberry Shortbread Bars **(see p141)**

### WARM TUMMY IN COLD WEATHER

**Day 1** Best warm from the pan: Apricot and Vanilla Semolina Porridge with Almonds **(see p28)**

**Day 2** Fills you up and makes you happy: Vegetarian Lahmacun with Tofu & Soured Cream, warmed up in the oven or microwave **(see p54)**

**Day 3** Fires you up: Chickpea Chilli with Basmati Rice **(see p84)**

**Day 4** Up off the couch: One-Pot Cheeseburger Chilli **(see p91)**

**Day 5** Hot off the grill: Honey Nut Waffles with Spelt and Cinnamon **(see p147)**

# SPEEDY LUNCH & DINNER IDEAS

The recipes in this book are not just suitable for your lunchbox: they can also save the day at home. You may be searching for quick, wholesome lunches for your children, a satisfying but speedy lunch for yourself at the weekend, or an easy recipe for a last-minute dinner guest.

## SPEEDY LUNCHES

**Herb Orecchiette** with Toasted Cauliflower, Almonds, and Parmesan **(see p102)**

**Courgette Campanelle** with Goat's Cheese and Thyme **(see p98)**

**Spaghetti with Spicy Lentil Bolognaise (see p107)**

**Chickpea Chilli** with Basmati Rice **(see p84)**

**Tofu Vegetable Ratatouille** with Couscous **(see p82)**

**Tomato Pilaf** with Feta and Coriander **(see p70)**

**One-Pot Cheeseburger Chilli (see p91)**

## A FINE 3-COURSE DINNER

**1** **A Kind of Waldorf Salad (see p58)**
This colourful salad is a real feast for the eyes! Arrange it decoratively on the plates, and then drizzle with the dressing shortly before serving.

**2** **Broccoli Bows with Sautéed Salmon and Dill (see p97)**
For this classy pasta you should sauté the fish so it isn't completely cooked through. This way it stays wonderfully juicy, even if it continues to cook a bit further in the sauce. Arrange on plates to serve, and sprinkle with freshly ground pepper and sprigs of dill.

**3** **Blueberry Coconut Waffles (see p147)**
The waffle mixture can be prepared in advance, then you can cook the waffles themselves when you're with your guests. It's fun and the whole room fills with the delicious smell of waffles – simply heavenly!

# OFFICE PARTIES,
## INTRODUCTIONS, BIRTHDAYS, AND FAREWELLS

Perhaps it's your birthday, or you're new in the office; maybe there's a new addition to the family, or you want to throw a little farewell party. There's no better way to express your happiness, appreciation, or affection on special occasions than with some home-cooked treats. All the recipes in this book are suitable takeaway options, so you're spoiled for choice. Here are a few of suggestions for salads, finger foods, and sweet treats, which can be made with minimal time and effort, even in larger quantities.

**Layered Salad** with Courgette, Rocket, and Feta **(see p111)**

**Rosemary and Olive Meatballs** with Fennel Tzatziki **(see p78)**

**Pumpkin and Pearl Barley Tabbouleh** with Tahini, Cranberries, and Pumpkin Seeds **(see p67)**

**Empanadas** (see pp120–21)

**Savoury Muffins** (see pp122–23)

**Pizza Pockets** (see pp118–19)

**Filled Muffins** (see pp150–51)

**Savoury Tartlets** (see p114)

**Cookies** (see p138)

# WE
# SAY
# THANK YOU!

For this book we had the generous support of such lovely people, who helped give our book soul. We are particularly grateful to Pilar's parents, Nina and Jürgen Schacher, who let us cook in their lovely kitchen week after week. Even though we regularly turned it into a giant scene of total devastation. Thank you so much, and apologies once more for the burnt-on muffin remains in the oven, the dough-covered kitchen cloths, and the accumulation of crumbs on the floor!

We must also thank all those folks who let us photograph them at their homes and workplaces, and who modelled for us: the enchanting Madleen Dörr from the erlebe wigner! store, Chris Krömer (better known as Krömerlein), who bravely modelled for us half naked and still made us laugh with his Krömsi charm, the uniquely photogenic Simon Spannig, the sugar sweet Madeleine Klein, Kät's mum Tina, Pilar's uncle Gerd for lending us his fantastic VW van, Andreas Haffner who modelled for us in the middle of the Mercedes Benz factory, David Häuser who has once again showed his boundless dedication, Pilar's great uncle Christian who even made his practice available for our sandwich, Kät's sister Barbara Dimitriadis, and of course the staff at Dorling Kindersley and everyone else who was involved in the creation of this book! THANK YOU!

Cleo the cat

# THE TEAM

Cloé the koala

Camus the cat

### WHO WROTE IT?

Katerina Dimitriadis, 25, ran a successful restaurant in Nuremberg for seven years along with her mother and sister. She has a masters in politics and bibliography and works as a freelance cook, author, and editor. She lives with her sugar sweet cat Camus in Nuremberg.

### WHO PHOTOGRAPHED IT?

Pilar Schacher, 27, after studying design, turned her focus to food and fashion photography. Nowadays she lives and works in Berlin and misses her cat Cleo, who lives in Gutzberg near Nuremberg.

### WHO DESIGNED IT?

Graphic design graduate Andrea Schindler, 29, actually lives in Berlin, but was touring around Australia while simultaneously working on this book. As a child Andrea also had a cat, but now she prefers koalas.

Penguin
Random
House

**British Edition**
**Editor** Kate Berens
**Translator** Alison Tunley
**Project editor** Kate Meeker
**Senior art editor** Glenda Fisher
**Jacket designer** Amy Keast
**Indexer** Marie Lorimer
**Pre-production producer** Tony Phipps
**Senior producer** Stephanie McConnell
**Managing editor** Stephanie Farrow
**Managing art editor** Christine Keilty

**German Edition**
**Text** Katerina Dimitriadis
**Photography** Pilar Schacher
**Food styling** Katerina Dimitriadis and Pilar Schacher
**Editing** Gerti Köhn
**Design** Andrea Schindler
**Repro** Farbsatz, Neuried/Munich
**Production** Christine Rühmer
**Production coordination** Katharina Dürmeier
**Production manager** Dorothee Whittaker
**Project support** Sarah Fischer
**Publishing manager** Monika Schlitzer

First British Edition, 2016
Published in Great Britain by Dorling Kindersley Limited
80 Strand, London WC2R 0RL

A CIP catalogue record for this book is available from the British Library.

ISBN 978-0-2412-4838-6

Printed and bound in China

All images © Dorling Kindersley Limited
For further information see: www.dkimages.com

A WORLD OF IDEAS:
**SEE ALL THERE IS TO KNOW**

www.dk.com